The Essex Village Book

D0415099

THE VILLAGES OF BRITAIN SERIES

Other counties in this series include

Avon

Bedfordshire

Berkshire

Buckinghamshire

Dorset

Gloucestershire

Hampshire

Hertfordshire

Kent

Oxfordshire

Shropshire

Somerset

Staffordshire

Suffolk

Surrey

East Sussex

West Sussex

Warwickshire

Wiltshire

Worcestershire

The Essex Village Book

Compiled by the Federation
of Essex Women's Institutes from notes
sent by Institutes in the County

with illustrations by Joan Bill

Published jointly by
Countryside Books, Newbury
and the FEWI, Chelmsford

First Published 1988

Countryside Books
3 Catherine Road
Newbury, Berkshire

ISBN 1 85306 013 5

Cover Photograph is of Clavering
taken by Andy Williams

Produced through MRM Associates, Reading
Typeset by Acorn Bookwork, Salisbury
Printed in England by J. W. Arrowsmith Ltd., Bristol

Foreword

Essex is one of England's larger counties. With its undulating countryside, sandy beaches, estuaries, marches and creeks it is a county of many contrasts.

It has a long and fascinating history and owes many of its attributes to the Roman, Saxon, Norman, Tudor and Georgian eras.

WI Members and friends have spent a great deal of time in research for this book, and gained enormous pleasure in finding out tales of the county's past.

Under each village heading there is a delightful cameo of village life past and present. I hope that readers will want to add to that which they have read by visiting our villages and share the unspoilt rural atmosphere of Dedham Vale, the heart of Constable Country, enjoy the timber framed and gracious Georgian red brick houses, examples of pargetting and thatched roofs etc.

A warm welcome awaits you, and we hope this book will give you a taste of the real Essex.

Jocelyn Need
Co-ordinator

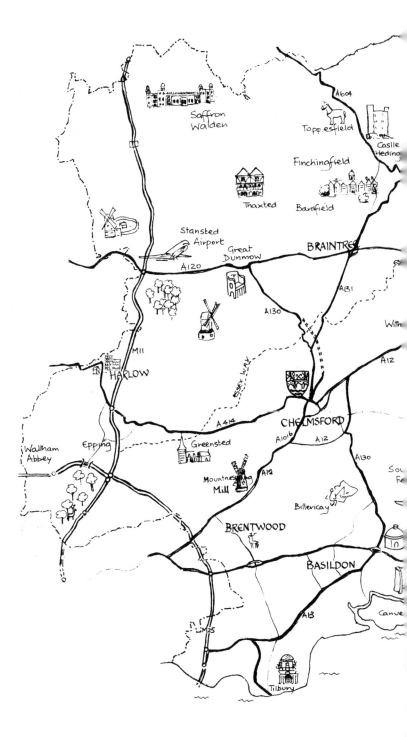

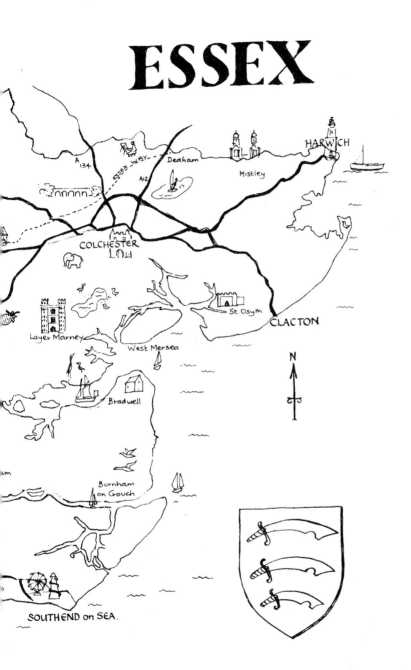

Acknowledgements

The Federation of Essex Women's Institutes would like to thank all Institutes whose members have worked so hard to provide material for this book. Also the following for assistance in providing material:

Miss W Beaumont (Wormingford)
Norman L Brunning (Manningtree)
Muriel Sanders (Galleywood)
Gilbert White (Fryerning)

Joan Bill of Epping for her county map and the charming line drawings.

Finally, a special thank you to Jocelyn Need, the co-ordinator for the project.

Abbess Roding 🖋

The village of Abbess Roding lies to the south of the main A414 road. It is an attractive village with some interesting buildings, including the medieval church of St Edmund. One building with a fascinating history is Anchor House.

Anchor House was once a public house of special character, being established by the chapel trustees as a respectable inn for refreshments for the congregation between services. The first publican was Isaac Reed who was keeping the inn in 1851 at the age of 75. In 1855 he was succeeded by Jacob Pavitt, in 1870 by William Westwood and in 1866 by John Parmenter.

During the time services were on in the chapel, no beer or other refreshments were consumed on the premises. The services were from 11 am–12.30 pm and 2 pm–3 pm. In between services lunch was served. The working class folk had theirs in the tap room. The lunch consisted of 2 pints of beer and a pennyworth of rolls and cheese. The rolls were made in the baker's shop which was run in conjunction with the inn. The gentry used a separate entrance, now the front door of the house. They took their lunch in a large upstairs room which reached across almost the whole of the inn. There were stables for a considerable number of horses and carriages and there were sometimes as many as 50 carriages.

The licence having ceased in 1910, Messrs Ridley sold the premises to Mr F. Parmenter. The inn sign, an iron anchor, was at one time removed but later presented to Mr Parmenter by Messrs Ridley. It still hangs over the front door.

The remains of the chapel were used by Mr Parmenter as piggeries and are still there today. The current owner of Anchor House is Mr R. Parmenter, great grandson of John Parmenter.

Aldham 🖋

Travellers on the A604, Cambridge to Colchester road, are probably too busy negotiating the hill, the bend, the bridge, the parked cars and avoiding juggernauts, to realise that they are passing through one of the prettiest village streets in North Essex.

But come to Aldham in June, on the 'Open Gardens' Sunday

and then visitors can really enjoy and appreciate the village. For several years now, about 20 gardens have opened their gates to the public. After weeks of hard work and loving care the moment arrives – and so do the visitors! Hundreds of them who, for a whole afternoon, wander round gardens of unimaginable contrast and beauty. Large landscaped gardens with vistas and tiny walled gardens; another full of ferns and yet another going back to Elizabethan times with elderflower cordial to sip in the shade.

Aldham church, standing at the crossroads at the top of the hill, its white spire topped by a golden weathercock, can be seen as a landmark for miles around. There is a great feeling of permanence about it, cool on a summer's day, the sunshine filling the chancel with light and colour. The church was built early in the 13th century and the porch, carved and beautifully moulded, added in 1330. There does not seem to be anything unusual in that; the point that people find hard to believe is that it was originally built a mile and a half away, right on the edge of the present village.

In 1854, after much discussion, deliberation and no doubt, argument the original church was pulled down to be rebuilt in a more central position. The existing materials were to be re-used and the cost, including the new stone spire, was only £1,477 – very difficult to find, even with grants and generous donations.

The Rev Charles Bannantyne, a determined and far-seeing man, was instrumental in rebuilding the church. He was a benefactor to the village, encouraging the school to be built, starting the library and also building four almshouses for the poor. A school and a road in Colchester pay tribute to another illustrious rector – the Rev Philip Morant – a great historian, most famous for his *History of Essex* published in 1768. Two great volumes are filled with the material that he gathered from 'The Best and Most Ancient Historians from Domesday Book Onwards'

Aldham Hall is the oldest house in the village, a medieval hall house steeped in history. The screens passage is still intact, the courtroom still exists and a priests' hole was found during renovation work. It is surrounded by lawns and box-edged gardens probably laid down in the reign of Queen Elizabeth I. There is a reference to a party being held on the lawns when oysters were eaten, so large that each one served several people! A former owner de Merk gave his name to the neighbouring village of Marks Tey.

In contrast to all that is old, there is 'Tranquillity', a very 20th century bungalow. Well designed, and unique, having asymetrical roofs and large windows, imagine the raised eyebrows when it was built! However, it is now as much a part of Aldham as any of the ancient houses, which were new themselves once upon a time.

Ardleigh 🌿

Ardleigh, on the main route from Colchester to Harwich, claims to be the largest Essex parish when the tide is in! (St Osyth being the other claimant.) One interpretation of Ardleigh is 'high pasture'.

Archaeological digs have proved that the village has been settled since Bronze Age times. One of the oldest houses in the centre of the village dates back to the 14th century. It is now called The Ancient House but was the Kings Head public house. The four manors of the village – Bovills, Martells, Piggotts (Ardleigh Hall, burnt down in 1979) and Moze – were used until recently by the local school as names for their teams.

A famous and influential inhabitant was Rev John Kelly, vicar of Ardleigh, who, in 1796, was afraid that the French might invade and the village be overrun. He visited all the farms and houses and made a list of all his parishioners. No other successful census was issued until 1841. Kelly is also noted for translating the Bible into Manx and it is said that when he was shipwrecked on his way to England from the Isle of Man he, like Caesar, held his manuscript in one hand high above his head so that it should not get wet.

Cannibal Jack – The true autobiography of a white man in the South Seas tells of the adventures and travellings of William Diapea, born at Ardleigh in the early 1800s. He traded amongst all the islands in the Pacific Ocean dealing with anything from muskets to pigs.

Ardleigh was affected by the great English earthquake on the morning of 22nd April 1884. Mr D. E. Cardinall, living at Bovill's Hall, reported that '. . . the walls of the room undulated, all the household were shaken rapidly from side to side as in a poor railway carriage on a badly laid line.' Two large chimneys at Crockleford Mills fell and local people who were indoors felt their houses were coming down.

11

The annual Ardleigh Garden Show, which used to be held in Newth Meadow, was always a big event and was famous for miles around. The Royal Eastern Counties Railway used to run special trains here. Farmworkers were given the day off to enjoy the fun of the fair, the marching displays, bands, athletics and the horticultural competition.

A more recent famous character in the village was Shedrach Sparling, the 'midnight baker'. He always began his round about 11 pm and when greeted with 'You're late!', replied 'No, I'm early. I should be here tomorrow morning.' The bakery, one of the last coal-fired bakeries using traditional tools and methods, was closed in 1986.

Arkesden 🐿️

Arkesden has been called 'the gem of the Essex Highlands'. People have lived here for thousands of years, bronze implements found here are now in the local museum. Saxons were settled here and after the Norman Conquest lands previously owned by Saxons were catalogued in the Domesday Book.

The village, surrounded at one time by dense woodland, was always a centre of agriculture. In medieval times it was mainly pastoral, but today there are no sheep, pigs and cattle, and farming now consists of arable crops. Several of the old farm names, such as Becketts, Chandwell and Hob's Acre, still survive.

Interesting buildings are The Green Man, formerly an inn and the oldest house in the village, which boasts a priest's hole; Sexton's, formerly a farm called 'Saxons'; Wood Hall (the manor house) which in Norman times was called 'Archesdana'; Jeffreys, the oldest freehold in the parish, and Becketts a Tudor house. A private house called The Ancient Shepherd used to be an alehouse. The church of St Mary the Virgin has a Norman font. An impressive memorial to the Cutte family dated 1592 bears traces of iconoclasm by Cromwell's men who were quartered in the district.

Local names which have survived for more than a hundred years are Bailey, Wombwell, Reed, Patmore, Dyer, Kemp and Pluck. The population of Arkesden has varied, in 1862 it was 506 and today it is 298. Many small cottages which housed a large family have been combined into larger ones, and there has been some new building, though there is some restriction of building as Arkesden is in a conservation area. Few farmworkers remain, many of the breadwinners commuting to London or neighbouring towns.

Only one ghost has been seen. There have been two sightings of an elderly lady at Wood Hall, probably Mrs Birch Wolfe, who had a feud with the vicar in the late 19th century!

Ashdon

Ashdon is derived from 'the ash tree on the hill'. At the top end of the village is a lovely old church dedicated to All Saints, the building of which was begun in the 11th century. A village settlement developed close to the church, but with the spread of the plague in the 14th century this settlement was abandoned for an alternative site at the bottom of the hill.

It is said that Henry VIII and Anne Boleyn were secretly married in All Saints church. Certainly one can be sure that, later on, Oliver Cromwell passed through during one of his campaigns. A room in the Rose and Crown public house still has the wall paintings by one of his followers in what is called the Cromwell Room.

In 1377 the Ashdon Guild (a religious guild) was founded and sometime between then and the late 15th century a hall called the Guildhall was built by the members, close to the church. Much later it became a workhouse and later still turned into three cottages. Now, however, it is attractively restored and is a private house.

In 1865 a branch railway was built in the outlying fields of the village, giving the community access to Saffron Walden, London and beyond in one direction or Haverhill, Cambridge, Norfolk etc in the other. Unfortunately it was closed in 1964, the lines taken up and the land once more is under cultivation.

Ashdon has two halls, each owned by a political party, one called the Conservative Club, the other the Labour Hall. Neither is entirely satisfactory any longer to meet the needs of the community. There is also a Baptist church – meetings first took place in a barn until the chapel was built, close to the centre of the village.

The 1801 census shows the existence of 39 separate farms in the parish of Ashdon. Many of these were still thriving before the First World War and manned by large numbers of farmworkers. Conditions for the workers were very poor at the beginning of the century, wages were 15 shillings per week. Matters reached a head in 1913 when the farmworkers went on strike. They demanded better working conditions and higher wages. Their action made itself felt for miles around. Eight Ashdon farmworkers served 14 days in Cambridge prison, rather than pay the fines asked of them. With the onset of war in 1914 the workers agreed to accept half of their wage demands and the 'North Essex Strike' came to an end.

With the need for less men working on the farms, many have moved away to find other employment. A lot of the cottages are now occupied by commuters and retired people.

Ashingdon ✎

Nine hundred years ago, when Canute decided to bring his fight for the kingdom with Edmund Ironside to an all out battle, he found the countryside of Essex on the Crouch river very flat. He must have wondered if he could gain any sort of advantage in a water meadow landscape. The battle commenced and quickly a foothold was established on a hill about a mile from the river. The date was 1016.

History tells that Canute defeated Edmund and the *Anglo Saxon Chronicle* reports that in 1020 the victor returned to consecrate a stone church and dedicate it to the souls of the slain. A silver coin of Canute has been found in the churchyard. Ashingdon church overlooks the village and the river Crouch, a guardian of long ago, but still the centre of village life. St Andrews Minster, as it is called, has a model Viking ship over the centre aisle and this brings many visitors and historians to enjoy the peace of a truly country church.

An hour's train ride from London, the village has attracted many commuters and new houses have sprung up to swell the community. The village school is a busy part of life, with an active PTA and youngsters from all parts of the country. The village also has a thriving hall where many clubs meet and enjoy social life.

Aveley 🌿

Since the Second World War, the character of Aveley has changed completely, but when reading any books about Aveley, and particularly the manor house of Belhus, it can be seen there is much to learn of its past history.

Belhus mansion, now demolished, stood in its own grounds close to Aveley village. It was originally a deer park and in the year 1327 Nicholas Bellhouse – hence the name – built the first house, believed to be of timber. In 1458, it changed hands and the Barrett family became the owners. In 1520 John Barrett changed the appearance of the house to the Tudor style, altering windows etc to the look many villagers still remember.

A Barrett descendant, Lord Dacre, commissioned Capability Brown to landscape the grounds in 1740 and to this day his pond still remains. Small farms owned locally, paid rent which was a source of income, together with the breeding of horses. Thomas Barrett, another descendant died in 1919 and consequently the contents of the house were sold in an eight day sale in 1923. Many older Aveley residents still remember the animal cemetery in the park surrounding the house. There were graves for mice, cats, dogs, horses, etc. Sir Thomas Barrett-Lennard was a great animal lover and it was he who ensured the animals had a serene resting place.

In the 16th century, Aveley had a market held in the High Street opposite the church gate. Also in much the same situation was an inn called Sign of the Harrow and there several men met to form a 'Lunatick Club' in 1763. This club provided a meeting place where members could chat and listen to information which rumour provided. Rules were drawn up, including fines for bickering, swearing and being drunk.

The church itself dates back to 1120 when work was begun on the building. Inside there are brasses of Radulphus de Knevynton who it is thought may have lived in a house on the site of the present Sir Henry Gurnett along Romford Road. Another brass commemorates Nathaniel and Elizabeth Bacon who died in 1588, being infant children of Edward Bacon. These brasses are well known and people travel from all over the country to see them. The Barrett-Lennard family are also laid to rest in the churchyard.

15

Barnston 🌿

The village of Barnston has a history going back thousands of years since men first came to live on this hilltop. In those terms, the Norman parish church is a fairly recent building. The history of the village has been researched by a familiar and popular man of the village, Harry de Caux.

The name of John Salmon of Barnston is synonymous with sugar-beet harvesters. He was born at Puttocks Farm in 1907 and by the time he was 16, he was managing 50 acres for his mother, after his father's death. He began agricultural contracting in the early 1930s, specialising in field drainage after the Ministry of Agriculture ceased to operate in the 1950s. A sugar-beet grower himself, he was disappointed in the quality of the machines and on Christmas Eve 1946 he launched his own mechanical lifter. During the next year he sold six machines. The modern Salmon Harvesters do the whole process of what used to be a cruel and back-aching job. More than 500 of the 'model 55' harvesters were sold.

Mr Salmon died in 1971. Local people remember him for his quiet generosity, for taking responsibility for building the Barnston village hall and founding Barnston Football Club.

Belchamp St Paul 🌿

The name Belchamp St Paul comes from the French 'beau champs', which means beautiful fields. It is still a beautiful chestnut tree-lined village, surrounded by fields. The St Paul part of the name is because the village was given to St Paul's Cathedral in 931 and remained largely ecclesiastical property until 1947. Knowle Green which is at one end of the village is named from knoll, meaning 'high point'. The green that end is enclosed by a hawthorne hedge which dates back to the Enclosure Act. There is a population of 300 people, made up largely of newcomers seeking peace and quiet from town life.

There has been one famous inhabitant during the history of this old village – namely Arthur Golding, who in Henry VIII's reign resided in Pauls Hall, at the back of the church. He was a classical scholar and translated plays from the Latin, which Shakespeare made use of. In fact, there are people who believe that he and his brother-in-law, the Earl of Oxford were the real authors of Shakespeare's plays. His descendants living in the USA presented a stained glass window in the parish church, dedicated in 1935. Unfortunately, this was badly damaged in the 1987 October gale.

St Andrew's church dates back to 1430 and is a large one for a small village. It stands about a mile from the main part of today's village, but it is said that originally the village was near the church, people moving away during the Great Plague. The choir stalls have misericords underneath which came from Clare Priory.

Up to the Second World War the majority of the men worked on local farms. There were some sheep and cows but it is mainly arable farming in this area.

Originally there was a forge, a shoemaker with three men working for him, a coffin maker and three bakers, namely Amos, Mantle and Crisps. The latter lived and worked at the mill. A descendant of the Crisps – 'Annie at the Mill', lived to be 100 years old and died on 7th February 1963. There were two grocer's shops, a separate post office, a wheelwright and four public houses. Now all that is left is one shop and combined post office and three public houses – The Half Moon, The Plough and The Cherry Tree.

There was a reading room on the village green, but this was pulled down at the end of the Second World War and replaced with the Pemberton Room, named after a former inhabitant of the village. He left money in his will for a charity to be paid to the poor of Belchamp St Paul and this continues to be done to the present day.

After the Pemberton Room, the village was presented with the present beautiful village hall called The Community House, by the Bryce family of Birdbrook, who were friends of the vicar. This was opened in 1951 and endowed for its upkeep. It is a reed thatched house, looking very much like a stately home.

In the 17th and 18th centuries, wives and children used to plait straw for the Luton hat industry, sitting on the doorsteps working in the summer.

Black Notley 🎐

Situated on the fringes of Braintree, Black Notley is a village proud of its identity. This is a name, along with its neighbour, White Notley, which arouses curiosity. It appears that after the Norman conquest the manor of 'Nutlea' came into the possession of Geoffrey de Mandeville, Earl of Essex and Roger Bigod, Earl of Norfolk. They founded the two churches, glebe lands and manor houses upon their own lands. Thus Black Notley and White Notley came into being.

The green lane which runs between the Witham and Chelmsford roads is the remnant of a Saxon road forgotten and unseen by the general public. There is evidence from old maps that a farmhouse and cottages once stood alongside this old highway. These have long since disappeared, the only living evidence of their existence is a luxuriant growth of bullace trees and oddments of bricks and tiles in the ground.

Today Black Notley is a busy place. The new Braintree by-pass cuts across its northern boundary. The large additional residential area of White Court has added to its population. The White Court estate itself has an interesting history, being once the manor of Oaklands which, along with the manor of Great and Little Slamseys, formed part of the endowment of Lees Priory and came within the ecclesiastical boundary of White Notley. This area was declared part of Black Notley after the Divided Parishes Act of 1889. In the early 1960s old cottages were demolished in the centre of the village and farmland purchased to make way for the Bedalls and Brain Valley estates.

The church dedicated to St Peter and St Paul is of Norman origin and has undergone many repairs and alterations over the centuries. Bombing in 1943 caused much damage and restoration was not complete until 1953. As a result the ancient stairs leading to the rood loft are exposed in the north wall. Today the church still stands in a peaceful oasis enhanced by the barn roofs and buildings of the 16th century manor house of Black Notley Hall.

The naturalist, John Ray, who is buried here, is Black Notley's most famous son. Born in 1627 at the village smithy, he went to school in Braintree and then on to Trinity College, Cambridge. His first book, a collection of proverbs, was built up from conversations during his early years. He discovered plants previously unrecorded in the lanes and hedgerows of Black Notley. The 300th anniversary of his most famous work *Historia Plantarum* was celebrated by a John Ray supper held in the village hall in 1986.

What of today's people in Black Notley? Several of the old families are still living here and seeing a very different scene to that of years ago. The hospital and other businesses such as building, shops, road haulage and three public houses give employment to many. Farming is still the most extensive industry, although the number of farmers has dwindled and many acres have been swallowed up by development.

Bobbingworth ஒ௸

Bobbingworth (commonly called Bovinger) was mentioned in the Domesday Book 1086. Situated approximately 2 miles from Ongar and 5 miles from Epping, the village with two names is unique in that it has never had a public house or a village street. The village consists of small groups of houses scattered amid arable farmland.

St Germaine's church derives its name from the French missionary turned soldier whose battle cry was 'Alleluia', some 1500 years ago. Now 'Alleluia' is the name given to the church magazine. The present building dates back to the 13th century and the list of rectors starts before 1276. The last resident rector left in 1981 and since then there has been a priest-in-charge residing at Fyfield.

Originally there was a wooden spire, this was replaced by the present stone tower in 1840, and six bells were installed at the expense of the Reverend William Oliver, who was the incumbent from 1838 to 1899. Because the tower is not high enough to accommodate the bells, they are rung from the porch, the congregation having to walk carefully through the ringers to enter the church door. There is seating for about 120 people in the high box pews which were installed at the expense of the Rev William Oliver in 1857.

Bovinger mill was shown on old maps as early as 1678. A three storied wooden post windmill with a brick roundhouse below ceased to work between 1912–14. Bread was baked in the ovens on the premises and sold in the mill shop as well as delivered to many local households by horse and cart until 1942. The Essex huffer, a three cornered roll, was a speciality. Sadly, Bovinger windmill was blown down during a heavy storm in 1923, and the roundhouse was subsequently demolished. The mill shop is now Bovinger post office.

Records show that there was a manor of Blake Hall in the 12th century. The estate was purchased by Capel Cure in 1789 and since that time Blake Hall has remained in the same family. In 1940 the RAF requisitioned the whole house. The south wing rooms have not been restored and now house items of RAF memorabilia.

A girls school was established in 1822 with support from Capel Cure of Blake Hall. By 1846 there were 24 girls attending. The only school for boys was the Sunday school. In 1846 Capel Cure built a school and teacher's house near the church. The school was closed in July 1959 and was later converted into a dwelling house.

Bocking 🌿

The earliest events of which there are records are in connection with the church. The present church on the original Saxon site was probably begun about the reign of Edward III, when the main aisle with its graceful pillars and arches, in the Decorated style, was built. A large part was added and the whole embellished in Tudor times, when the wool trade was flourishing and money was plentiful. The church is built mainly of flint and is a fine example of its kind. The small turret on the tower which gives a special character to it, is a later addition of the 18th century.

The deanery at Bocking has received many distinguished visitors in its day. William Wordsworth stayed there with his brother, and may have composed a poem under the shade of its beautiful trees. The most honoured guest was undoubtedly the exiled King of France, Louis XVIII, who in 1808, accompanied by his suite, dined with Lord Charles Aynsley, the then Dean.

The famous Bocking bells are eight in number. The tenor bell is reputed to have the most musical note in Essex and weighs just under a ton, one of the heaviest in the country.

Messrs Courtaulds' silk factory was the chief feature of Bocking, employing hundreds of hands and famous for its output throughout the world. The first enterprise of this firm in Bocking was the purchase of the old Baize watermill in 1819. They already had mills at Pebmarsh, a mill north of Halstead, where they had started 20 or 30 years earlier, and at Braintree where an old flour mill on the river had been purchased in 1809. The silk industry took the place of the old wool industry, and went from strength to strength. The large factory at Bocking dates from various periods since the 19th century.

Old inhabitants remember how 60 and more years ago little girls of 12 went to work from 6 am to 6 pm, for a wage of three shillings a week, and the brighter ones soon rose to good positions.

In the 19th century the factory was chiefly concerned with the manufacture of black crepe, some secret process of crimping being an important feature. With the disuse of crepe for mourning, business was not so good, but the increased use of silk fabrics of all kinds and the discovery of artificial silk more than restored the fortunes of Bocking.

The oast house at Bocking

21

The rivalry of Braintree and Bocking is of long standing shown by an old rhyme, which John Ray in 1660 (as he walked up Hoppit Hill) heard the boys of Braintree singing to the disparagement of Bocking.

> Braintree boys, brave boys,
> Bocking boys – rats!
> Church Street – puppy dogs!!
> High Garrett – cats!!!

After many years of disagreement and controversy, the twin communities are now united in one Urban District of Braintree and Bocking, but Bocking still holds onto its individuality.

Boreham 🐚

There is evidence of Roman occupation in Boreham and the old A12 was once a Roman road leading from London to Colchester.

It was in Saxon times that the village got its name, and one theory is that since 'bore' was a Saxon word for market, it could once have been a market town. Boreham is mentioned in the Domesday Book and its importance at that time is indicated by the fact that its annual value to the kings revenue was equal to that of Chelmsford. The parish was divided into six manors: Old Hall, New Hall, Calwaltes (Culverts), Walkfares, Brent Hall and the manor of Porters.

The church is of Saxon origin and some Saxon work still remains. It has a Norman tower which was added later. It is unique in Essex in that it is the only one remaining with a central tower. The tower is Norman but after the first 15 feet there is an arch made of Roman brick.

The Sussex Chapel was built in the late 16th century as a tomb for the Earls of Sussex, who were given the manor of New Hall by Elizabeth I. The Tyrell family of Boreham House also have their own vault at the back of the church.

New Hall is mentioned in the Chelmsford Hundreds as having one of the finest avenues of lime trees in the kingdom. It originally belonged to Waltham Abbey, being given to them in 1062. Then in 1350 the canons exchanged it for manors nearer Waltham Abbey.

Under Henry VI and Margaret of Anjou, it became Crown property and was to know, in the years that followed, Lancastrian and Yorkist ownership according to the fortunes of the rival houses. Finally, when a victory on Bosworth Field in 1485 brought Henry VII to the throne he granted New Hall to Thomas Boteler, Earl of Ormond. Then through the marriage of Ormond's daughter it was inherited by the Boleyn family. From Sir Thomas, Ann Boleyn's father, Henry VIII acquired New Hall in 1517. He enlarged and beautified the palace. Delighted with it he called it Beaulieu.

Boreham House was built in 1728 for Benjamin Hoare, on land which was once part of the New Hall estate. He had sold New Hall to build for himself this smaller house. It changed hands several times, until it was bought by Sir John Tyrell who owned and lived in Boreham House around 1810.

Bradfield 🐟

Into this small peaceful agricultural community, on the estuary of the river Stour, there came in the year 1871, the Rev Leighton G. Hayne, DMus, to be rector of the 13th century church of St Lawrence, and thereby to disturb its peace.

He brought with him, in ten large railway trucks, a five-manual organ and massive wooden pipes, later referred to as 'Hayne's tubs'. Another story says that they came by sailing barge to the hard at Jacques Hall. Among the pieces for this organ was an instrument from St Albans Abbey, which had come from the church of St Dunstan-in-the-East, London and probably dated back to the 17th century. He was striving to outdo the organ at the Albert Hall, which, recently completed by its builder Willis, was claimed by him to be the largest in the world.

His plans to instal such a monster organ in the little church met with opposition on the grounds that considerable damage would be caused. But Dr Hayne was not deterred, and in great secrecy, with the help of a village builder, undertook the work himself.

The whole operation was a disaster for the chancel. A chamber for the organ was built onto the north wall, but there was nowhere for the massive pipes – the Hayne's tubs – and these were placed horizontally in a cavity under the floor, which was ruthlessly removed. Stone slabs and monumental brasses were pulled up, the latter being transferred to the south wall except for a few loose ones which later disappeared. The vibrations and disturbance caused by the organ when it was played, necessitated repairs to the roof, and the insertion of an iron tie-bar across the chancel

When once in use, the parishioners gradually began to appreciate the new organ, and when part of it was taken to Mistley to form the nucleus of the organ in the new church there, they were considerably annoyed.

Eighty years passed before the chancel floor was restored as nearly as possible to its state before Dr Hayne's excavations. In 1958 the Earl of Verulam, a descendant of the Grimston family, whose memorial brasses had been removed, initiated the detailed work of re-locating his ancestors' tombs, and repairing the damage done to the chancel. In 1962 the organ, which was in a very poor condition, was also restored.

Bradwell-on-Sea ✑

Bradwell-on-Sea is probably best known for its 7th century Saxon chapel of St Peter but there are a remarkable number of items of interest to be found here. The chapel was built right at the edge of the marshes by St Cedd, a missionary who had converted the East Saxons. He chose this remote site for his principal church, which he constructed from the masonry of the Roman coastal fort of Othona in whose gateway it now stands.

The strange yellow and red pyramids on the saltings are not bird hides, but direction markers. These were used with the nearby watch tower to guide planes using the bombing range, out to their targets on the mud flats. Another relic of this range, which operated from 1938 to the early 1960s, can be seen in the front playground of the village school. A section of the target service pier, its rail lines and one of the trolleys has been rebuilt there.

Opposite to the school is Cage Row, an attractive terrace of timber framed cottages. The name is derived from the square, brick built cage or lock up, that stands at the corner of the churchyard. This parish prison would have housed the drunks or felons, before they were brought up before the magistrate. Its last occupant is said to have been a suspicious looking foreigner who foolishly had wandered into Bradwell during the First World War. Another little gem can be found at the churchyard gate. A mounting block, or 'jossing' block to assist riders to mount or dismount from their horses.

The church, dedicated to St Thomas, dates from the 14th century but it has been much altered through the centuries. The chancel is of the earliest date, the nave having been rebuilt in 1706 and the tower in 1743. The fine 14th century timber porch is oddly enough, a modern addition. It was placed here in 1957 when its original home, Shopland church near Southend, was demolished.

In the village centre many of the houses, despite their Georgian brick facades date back much earlier. White Lyons hides a fine timber framed home behind its elegant frontage. The same is true of neighbouring New Hall. Look out for the cast iron advertising plaques that are displayed on the old smithy. The village hall was designed by the architect of London's Savoy Hotel, Arthur Heygate Macmurdo, a leading member of the Art Nouveau movement.

Bradwell is really a collection of villages. The Waterside has grown around the safe anchorage in Bradwell Creek with the adjacent marina providing further facilities for boat owners. The stately fleet of Thames sailing barges, that once sailed from here, have been replaced by a wide variety of yachts and motor craft.

Overlooking the estuary and the Waterside is Bradwell Power Station, one of the first commercial nuclear generating stations to be built in Britain. Construction began in 1957 and power was raised in 1961.

Braintree

The large and busy community of Braintree has managed to retain a sense of individuality which is the basis of village life.

Occupations here are very varied and have grown tremendously since the coming of the railway in 1848. In the last century Courtaulds silk mills, Warners and Son (where silks and velvets were woven for Coronations and Royal weddings), Crittall and Company (famous for their windows, etc.,) Lake & Elliots and Bradbury's, both engineering firms, provided much employment. Courtaulds are no more, but one of their first factories is now in use as part of the Tesco Garden Centre.

The most famous past event must have been the annual fair, granted by charter by King John in 1199. A weekly market was also granted, and this has become more important and is a regular event, although the fair has disappeared. Another interesting feature was the Company of Four & Twenty who governed for 200 to 300 years, and was composed of self-elected members, a system peculiar to Braintree.

The most important building must be the Town Hall, one of many Courtauld gifts, built between 1926 and 1928. It is surmounted by a bell tower with a clock, above which stands a bronze figure representing Truth. The Council Chamber on the first floor is panelled with oak and holly. Paintings around its ceiling represent scenes from the history of Braintree. These murals and others in the chairman's room, were painted by Maurice Greiffenhagen, RA. The building is now a Heritage, Arts, Meeting and Tourist Information Centre for the benefit of the community.

St Michael's church, has Roman connections and a fine spire, perhaps a landmark for the pilgrims passing through for many centuries. There are also ancient buildings, such as The Swan Inn, and The Constitutional Club (with Tudor gables at the rear). The finest old houses are those situated in Bradford Street, the reminders of a famous woollen industry, which ended about 1800.

On the front of the old Six Bells Inn, in Bradford Street, is Old Harkelees, said to come down from his perch to bathe in the river – a story told to persuade children to go to sleep!

The local word 'gant' should also be mentioned, as it is used only in Braintree, and is the word for an alley, two of which are situated in the ancient market place, between Bank Street and Dury Lane, and between High Street and Sandpit Lane.

Brightlingsea 🦢

There are only two approaches to Brightlingsea, which lies on the coast roughly 10 miles from Colchester and 12 from Clacton. One, by sea, and the other by the only road which winds into the town to reveal a view of fields, the creek and All Saints church – a well-known landmark affectionately referred to by its inhabitants as 'The Old Church'. It once nestled amongst tall Scotch firs, but since the night of the hurricane on 16th October 1987 now stands starkly at the top of the hill.

Originally this church stood within easy reach of the hall and the manor house and its village, but during the plague the villagers fled to the waterside and set up its community. Today, with the growth of the town it is gradually creeping back to its church.

Around the interior of the church are 206 tiles, each commemorating the loss at sea of its seamen and inhabitants since 1872. The tower rises to 100 feet and has corner pinnacles. It was this tower that Canon Pertwee used to climb in adverse conditions to display a lantern to guide the ships to port, and it is in the belfry that the ceremony of Choosing the Deputy takes place on the Monday following St Andrew's Day. Brightlingsea is a 'limb' of the Cinque Port Liberty of Sandwich and the Deputy swears his oath of allegiance to the Mayor of Sandwich.

In the High Street is Jacobe's Hall, built about 1250. Jacobe, the original owner became, on the death of his third wife Matilda, the first priest of Brightlingsea. The hall is unique in that due to the work of the Beriffe family in the early 14th century it is possible for the visitor, by climbing the tower steps, to come breast high with the king beam and the king post, the wood of which is estimated to be over 900 years old and cut from local timber.

An American gentleman, Mr Bayard Brown spent a considerable amount of time aboard his steam yacht in the harbour and presented the town with its Recreation Ground, and a peal of ten tubular bells (in 1889) to be found at All Saints church. Likewise, another eccentric, Mr Bateman constructed a folly on the Western Promenade which remains to this day.

The town has strong nautical connections, its two large ship-yards produced many fine yachts and ships, and its inhabitants fine captains and crews. There are still some senior ladies in the town bearing unusual names bestowed upon them by proud seafaring fathers equally proud of their ships, after whom they were named! Once famous for its oysters, the industry suffered through severe weather in the 1950s. The ceremony of dredging the first oysters was held in the creek with visiting dignitaries aboard, and the Oyster Feast is held in Colchester to this day.

Walk down to the waterside area and the character is evident. Cottages built for fishermen and crewmen, larger houses for the captains. One street of nice houses is alleged to have been nick-named 'Mistresses Row' and housed the lady friends of certain captains!. Pause a while on The Hard, get chatting to a genuine old 'local' and the yarns abound!

Brightlingsea's link by rail fell under the Beeching axe despite local protestations. Today the site houses the community centre and a caravan site and it is possible to take a pleasant walk along the creek edge on a route once traversed by the steam train known as The Crab and Winkle.

Bulphan 🌿

Sitting like a top hat on Thurrock, Bulphan has borders with Basildon, Brentwood and Havering and is easily missed altogether as you travel from The Halfway House to the Orsett Cock. Ye Old Plough House Motel places it on the map for some, but most residents of Bulphan (past and present) have been happy to be off the beaten track.

At the time of the Domesday Book, Bulgenen as it was then (meaning marshland by a fortified place) had a large number of sheep, from whose milk cheese was made. Pinkerton's farm standing on the A128 is still called Wick Place to denote this.

The main village at the turn of this century stretched from the church of St Mary the Virgin, past the school and rectory, centring on the post office, coal merchant and Went's bakery at China Lane and continuing to the Harrow pub, where Bill Thomas was the stonemason.

The Fen was enclosed by three Fengates. Villagers had grazing licences and Fred Jiggens still has his licence entitling him to keep 2½ sheep there! As the Fen was marshy and wet, it was the custom to run any geese through a puddle of tar, and then sand, to 'waterproof' their feet. The local sport was quoits and as the quoit-ground in front of the forge was often a quagmire, the men from the Harrow would sometimes take off their heavy workboots in order to keep their footing. These two facts combined led to surrounding villages considering Bulphan folk queer as they shod their geese and went barefoot themselves!

Farmworkers' children who lived near the Fengates would listen out for horses whilst they were carrying out their daily chores and run to open the gate, saving the driver from climbing down and usually earning a penny which would be spent on a 1d bar of Sharp's toffee at Mrs Thomas' tuckshop at the Harrow.

With the railway to East Horndon arrived the weekend and holiday Londoners. They bought plots and put up huts. With the Second World War, many of these families built more substantial homes and moved into the village permanently. There is a parallel today with the self-build plots that are a prominent feature of Bulphan now.

The Fen has always been a damp, misty and mysterious place. During the First World War, Mr Walford the gravedigger and his family failed to turn into their gateway at Stone Hall, and ended up – pony, trap and all – in the Mardyke by the Harrow Bridge. Even today, many drivers misjudge that same bend in the fog and end up nose-down in the Mardyke!

A distinctive feature of Bulphan are the water-pumps outside the council houses in Church Road: these are artesian wells and Lesley Read-Andrews of Pear Tree Corner did the well-boring.

Fred Jiggens of the Fen has written a book tracing the development of the faith of the Peculiar People in Essex, and has also achieved some fame as a speaker of true Essex dialect: his tapes may be heard in Colchester Museum.

Canvey Island 🌿

Canvey Island is situated in the Thames estuary near Southend, separated from the mainland by a creek. After Roman occupation in the 1st and 2nd centuries AD, there is a long history of tenacious Anglo-Saxon farmers who raised sheep on the higher parts of the island, though constantly threatened by flooding from the sea at high tide.

In the 17th century local landowners engaged a Dutch engineer named Cornelius Vermuyden, who was engaged on other enclosure work throughout the Thames estuary and Fen areas, to build the first sea walls. He carried out the work employing many Dutch workmen, some of whom stayed on after the work was completed. Permission was given them by the king to build a church so that they could worship in their own tongue.

The oldest building on the island today is said to be the Lobster Smack inn, mentioned by Charles Dickens in his novel, *Great Expectations*. Two Dutch cottages still exist, octagonal in shape with high conical thatched roofs. One cottage is privately owned and still occupied, the other is a museum.

In the last century the Reverend Hayes became the first resident minister on the island. He built a church dedicated to St Katherine, using materials including the porch and windows of the previous building. He also built a vicarage and the first school on the island. His other venture was to sink a well for fresh water. St Katherine's church is now redundant and has become a Heritage and Conservation centre. A new church, dedicated to St Nicholas, has been built further along the road.

Residential increases and the advance of popularity of Canvey as a holiday resort, especially for the Eastenders of London, meant that urgent improvements were necessary. A new main road from the ferry to the eastern end of the island was constructed in 1928 and work started on the first bridge to span Benfleet Creek, which was officially opened in 1931. With this came a rash of bungalow estates and Canvey ceased to be a rather quaint, off-beat community (with, let it be admitted, a somewhat dubious reputation) and began developing into another dormitory area for London.

In 1953 Canvey hit the headlines when it suffered in the calamity of the East Coast floods. The Red Cow public house became the headquarters of the army, who came to rescue the trapped inhabitants and repair the sea wall. Their efforts were successful and later the pub was re-named the King Canute, the place where the tide was ordered out.

One might have expected such a calamity to be the death-knell of the area, but with the strengthening of the sea defences the community went from strength to strength. The population is now about 40,000, a far cry from the bungalow/shanty town atmosphere of the 1920s.

The Chignalls ༝༖

There were formerly three parishes, Chignall St James, Chignall St Mary and Chignall Smealy. Chignall St. James has had many different versions of its name. In 1542 it was known as Chickney

St James, in 1575 as Chicknell St James, and was sometimes referred to as Great Chignall.

Chignall St James' church and St Mary's church both dated back to the 1300s. St Mary's was pulled down long ago and St James' church took over the parish of St Mary's as well. A number of years ago St James' church was sold and permission was given for it to be turned into a private dwelling, alterations and repairs began in 1987.

Chignall Smealy, way back in 1564, was known as Smely Chygnal, it was also known as Little Chignall. Chignall Smealy church of St Nicholas dates back to the 16th century. The tower, nave, chancel and vestry are of Tudor brickwork and there is also a brick font. The parish was sometimes referred to as Brick Chignall. At one time there were just two sources of employment, agriculture and brick making, the brickfields being situated at Chignall Smealy, down the Shore Road, as it was known at the time. There was a considerable seam of brick clay and the bricks were made and baked in a small kiln at the side of the road. A number of the older houses in Chignall were built from the bricks made locally.

Chignall Smealy, at one time, boasted a post office and general stores, but sadly that is closed now, and that goes for the village school as well. There is a lovely cricket field, which in 1987 won a Gifford Award for Best Kept Playing Field. There were 2 black-smiths in the area, one at Chignall Smealy and one at Chignall St James. Bearmans at Chignall St James was blacksmith, wheel-wright and local undertaker.

The Three Elms at Chignall St James was an old inn, and the Pig and Whistle at Chignall Smealy was an old beer house. No ladies were allowed in to drink, and the men used to look out of the windows to 'peek and whistle' the girls. That was the original name for the pub, but somewhere along the line it was changed to Pig and Whistle.

In the very dry summer of 1974 it became known that a Roman villa had been situated at Chignall St James. First observed from the air as cropmarks, top soils were removed and archaeologists moved in. A complete skeleton of a horse's head and various joints of other animals and some well preserved tiles from the floor were found. There is a preservation order on the area now. Chignall St James is now a place for extensive gravel working.

A few villagers still work in the agricultural side of the village, but many trades are now represented in the community and most residents commute to work.

There are several old farms and houses in the area. Pengy Mill old water mill was Painge Mill Farm in 1777. Grays Farm dates back to 1777, Chessins to 1797 and Chignall Hall to 1564.

Chigwell Row 🌿

Chigwell Row lies on the border of Hainault Forest, a survival of the once extensive Royal Forest of Essex, where kings hunted as far back as Norman times. The village is mentioned in the Domesday Book as Cingheuuella or King's Well. There were many water springs in the area; the last known use of the mineral waters was in 1800.

The height of the village above sea level is 280 feet, which gave fine views of the Thames Valley before the area became so built up. This view is still available to those brave enough to climb the church tower when it is open on Flower Festival days in August.

Many would come in the past in char-a-bancs from London for a country outing. Their refreshment was provided by the many front room tea shops in the cottages. Those requiring alcoholic beverages would frequent one of the public houses, the most well known of which is The Maypole.

The Savill family, landowners, lawyers and much besides, lived in a 17th century building known as Woodlands, now Woodview Old Folks Home. In 1922 Philip Savill left £1,000 for gifts for the deserving poor. In 1950 the remaining £25 was distributed among the 12 most needy parishioners. Another benefactor, John Crowfoot, left £500 in 1903 for distribution of coal at Christmas to the poor of All Saints parish. This also was so reduced by 1950 that it was finally used to buy coal for 22 people.

All Saints church, a fine stone-dressed building, was consecrated in 1867. The western porch, much appreciated in wet weather, made an impressive building for what was then a small village community. Before this villagers used the chapel, which is now the United Reformed church. In 1831 a day school was started (2d per pupil per day). In 1839 a more permanent school was built near Millers Lane, but after a fire in 1885 it was rebuilt in red brick. In the 1830s a dame school and Sunday school existed opposite the recreation ground. The two bungalows there now have the original doors from the Sunday school.

There are a few wooden cottages left in the village. The timber for these was re-used from barns which had been storehouses for grain etc during the Napoleonic wars. Other timber from the Forest was used for ship-building in the 17th and 18th centuries and in 1775 2000 trees were ordered to be converted into charcoal for the powder mills at Barking and Enfield. One of the earliest trades mentioned in the baptismal records of All Saints church is 'charcoal burner'.

There was once a village blacksmith, the forge building being used by a plant nurseryman in recent times.

One local story has it that John Roger Arnold of Manchings, Gravel Lane, helped to win the Battle of Trafalgar. In fact he was a watchmaker who improved the action of the chronometer used in navigation at that time. His foreman, Thomas Prest, also started a business in Chigwell Row in 1821 and patented the 'attached winding movement' of watches as opposed to the detached key.

In a press report of 1828, an illegal fight was recorded between Tom Sweeney and Ned Savage in a secluded spot in the Forest, near the Maypole for £5 a side. In the *28th* round Savage fell and could not rise again. His seconds had to give in for him.

Childerditch & Little Warley ༺

To the south of Brentwood lie the villages of Childerditch and Little Warley, where the traveller comes to the ridge overlooking a wild and lovely common. Gorse covered and an area popular for picnic parties during warm weather, remote, secretive and desolate during the winter, this is the common of Little Warley and Childerditch.

Looking across the common to the hollow below the visitor would scarcely realise that these were villages he was seeing as there are no shops and no village street, and although the old village school still stands, with the school bell on top, this is now the village hall. In fact this is really a typical example of a Saxon village.

Mentioned in the Domesday survey of 1086, Little Warley (then

33

known as Warley Parva to distinguish it from its neighbouring village of Great Warley) and Childerditch (possibly named after the stream which runs through the village) are so closely integrated that it is hard to say where either village begins and ends.

There are a few whitewashed cottages of lathe and plaster, red brick or black and white Essex weatherboard, and clusters of brick farmhouses and buildings, the names of which have been handed down over the years. Whitehouse Farm, as an instance, is a protected building, known to be over 300 years old and having two Norman chimneys; during building work there in 1987 a William III coin was found. These old buildings are intermingled with some modern properties.

In a commanding position at the bottom of the common stands the much enlarged public house The Greyhound. Until 1796 this was known as The Bull and was kept by the lord of the manor and there is evidence that there was always a wayside inn there.

On the site of the old school house have been erected three bungalows. These have been funded by the 17th century Hugh Chappington Charity.

The little church of All Saints and St Faith at Childerditch was rebuilt in 1869, the original church having been destroyed by fire. This older church is described as 'having a steeple of brick at the bottom and timber above that, with a spire shingled'. The 14th century font escaped the fire and there is also an ancient lectern of uncertain age.

The parish church of St Peter in Little Warley is a patchwork building showing work of many centuries. It seems that the roof was thatched until about the last century as there is still much debris of such a roof under the present tiles.

The chancel dates back to the 16th century and the tower two centuries later. Somewhere about 1600 the whole of the nave and chancel appears to have been filled with box pews, in fact they still form the only seating accommodation, designed with care and still in excellent condition.

Beside the church stands Little Warley Hall, an early 16th century brick house, originally moated, with delightful grounds (now much smaller than the original house). In 1642 the Hall was acquired by the Royalist, Sir Denner Strutt, who, with the first of his four wives is commemorated by monuments on either side of the altar of the church.

In 1742 the Seven Years War brought a military camp to Warley. Eventually a barracks was built which was, for many years, the headquarters of the Essex Regiment. From about 1840 to 1860 Warley Barracks was owned by the East India Company and many of their old soldiers lie buried in the churchyard of St Peter's church. Indeed, the church was regarded for a long time as the parish church for the barracks, the soldiers marching down to the church for services.

The Barracks have now been demolished and the huge office block of Fords now stands in their place. Sadly too, the village has been transversed by the A127 Southend Road.

Clavering 🐝

The drainage of the Fens, and the taming of the Lee valley by locks and weirs, have diminished the river Stort and Wicken Water to tiny streams which are today little more than flood ditches: but even now the occasional wet period serves to remind us that they can quickly revert to the much more formidable barriers to communication that they must have been for much of the year in Saxon times. It was here at Clavering that one Robert Fitz Wymarc established one of the first 'Norman' castles in the kingdom – actually before the invasion of 1066. Some authorities believe that it was one of the places of safety to which Normans and other foreigners retired during the times of trouble between the death of the Confessor and the Norman Conquest.

All that remains of the castle is an extensive system of earthworks surrounding the square moated compound where the keep once stood. It is noticeable that the older parts of the village are sited round the rim of the original castle bailey, which remains as an undeveloped green central core to the village, some 8 acres in extent. The castle which gave birth to the village still dictates its layout.

Clavering is really a cluster of hamlets, or 'Greens', some 11 of them, covering an area of about 4000 acres in all. The population at the last census was just over 1000, but since then more houses have been added, the birthrate is up, and the count will now be nearer 1500. The transition from a mainly agricultural community to a well mixed cross section of businesses, trades and occupations has seemed relatively smooth. There is an excellent village store, comprising grocer, butcher, off licence and post office. There is a hairdresser, a garage/filling station and 3 pubs – one with a noted restaurant attached.

Clavering church was built about the end of the 14th century, replacing an earlier foundation which may have been the castle chapel. The church itself is very fine and large. There are some very interesting monuments, and the windows contain some of the finest medieval stained glass in Essex. Associated with the parish is an unusual charitable bequest – 'A barrel of whit herrings, and a cade of red, in Lent, issuing out of a farm called Valence'. This has long been converted into a sum of money, but Herring Charities are rare, and only few villages were once so endowed.

Church End, with its ancient Guildhall, is one of the most photographed and painted scenes in Essex. The Old House between the Guildhall and the road contains some fine murals and some interesting panelling. It was once the home of the Barlee family, whose monuments are prominent in the church. Another sight that will be familiar to many is Middle Street, with its ford, its row of picturesque cottages and the distinctive roofline of The Old Post-house at the top end.

Between these two, and secluded in its grounds is the oldest house in the village, The Bury. Pleasant but unremarkable from the outside, recent investigations have shown it to be an aisled hall manor dating from the 13th century. It, like the newly reconverted Guildhall and the Old House, is now a private residence.

Village societies flourish and the village hall, which started life as a very modest timber and board structure 50 years ago is now a thriving social centre. Each year there is a major Art Show at Easter when artists and craftsmen and women from a wide area exhibit their skills.

Cricket is played on Hill Green, and at Queen Elizabeth's Silver Jubilee an additional playing field, previously loaned through the generosity of a local farmer, was acquired for the village in perpetuity. The village has several times carried off the shield for the best kept large village run by the county.

Coggeshall 🌿

Coggeshall, although considered to be a village by many local people, was once a prosperous wool town situated on the river Blackwater, and stands on the line of the old Roman road, Stane Street.

It contains many fine historical buildings, including Paycocke's House, St Peter ad Vincula church, 12th century St Nicholas chapel, which was part of the Cistercian abbey which once stood close to the abbey mill, the Grange tithe barn, restored in 1984, and a wealth of timbered houses and Victorian cottages.

The manufacture of woollen cloth declined in 1800 and was replaced by the making of silk thread. In 1851 tambour lace was a thriving industry, also straw plaiting for hats. Seed growing has continued to the present day and supplies a large export market.

To the north of the village lies Marks Hall, a large estate on which once stood a mansion occupied by the Honywood family in the 17th/18th century. The public are allowed to walk around the paths and also through the surrounding woods, which contain many ancient trees.

In the 1840s the people of Coggeshall and district, were kept in a state of continual alarm by the daring and ruthless activities of a gang of men known for miles around as the Coggeshall Gang.

The gang's leader was an ostler called William Crow who prided himself on his smart appearance. Their headquarters was a public house in Stoneham Street called The Black Horse, now a private house. A policeman unsuccessfully searched these premises but on entering an empty property nearby he saw the leader sitting on a beam in the roof space. He went for help but on returning found the miscreant had fled.

He was finally arrested by a sharp eyed, plain clothes Metropolitan police sergeant whilst he was boarding a steampacket bound for America. Two other gangsters were captured by constables from Witham who travelled to Liverpool and arrested them on board ship bound again for America.

As a result of the trial one of the gang received a sentence of death, several others were transported for a number of years and the leader for the remainder of his life. One of the gang returned to Coggeshall after his period of transportation, quite comfortably off, having done well for himself abroad.

At last the citizens of Coggeshall could rest easy in their beds and in 1885 *The Chelmsford Chronicle* said 'For persons without superfluous cash who wish to pass a thoroughly restful holiday beyond the sound of the railway whistle Coggeshall is the very place'.

Cold Norton ❧

At first sight, Cold Norton is a very ordinary village, no picturesque village green, no charming cottages clustered around an ancient church. You can drive through it and hardly notice it. And yet, this undistinguished place has a long history. It was mentioned in the Domesday Book under the name of Nortuna, but remained a very small village and had only 173 inhabitants even at the beginning of this century. It grew considerably with the arrival of the railway, but the bulk of its development dates from the early 1960s.

Saint Stephen's church stands on the hill beside Norton Hall. The present building replaces the 12th century church which fell into disrepair, and was built at his own expense in 1855 by the rector, William Holland. (He was fortunate in having a wealthy wife!) Portraits of William and Mathilda Holland can be seen in the church. That of Mathilda shows Cold Norton church in the background. The rebuilding must have taken place with some urgency as the last service in the old church was at Easter 1855 while the new church was dedicated in time for Christmas the same year. The brasses and plate from the old church were transferred to the new and the lectern was constructed from its oak beams. Church records dating back to 1539 are still preserved.

Another notable landmark in Cold Norton is the great white water tower, built in 1967 and visible for many miles around. It was a boon to the villages, as, before its construction, in dry summers the water in the taps was reduced to a feeble trickle. Old people who remember the days before piped water recall having to trudge four miles for a cup of water in dry periods.

Cold Norton lost its railway in 1953 and the site of the station is now occupied by Greentrees Avenue, though the commuters who trek to North Fambridge each morning sorely regret the severing of the rail link.

In recent years Cold Norton has become more and more a quiet residential village, and yet it has mysterious qualities. Many people speak of an inexplicable urge to live here and a surprising number have moved away, only to return after a few years, unable to settle anywhere else.

Another mystery is the unusual fertility of this place. A stranger to the village cannot fail to notice the number of babies and small children, the ever-expanding school and thriving playgroup and mother and toddler club. Census figures reveal that Cold Norton has a higher birthrate than any of the surrounding villages.

Various theories have been put forward to explain these mysteries, but the most convincing one is the ancient belief that ley lines (the lines of magnetic force in the earth's crust) affect fertility. Several leys pass through Cold Norton. In prehistoric times fertility rites were conducted at standing stones or stone circles which marked the places where ley lines crossed.

It is intriguing to think that the earth's powers may go on working in our modern scientific age and goes to prove that a village should not be judged by its nondescript modern appearance. It may have links with an ancient, magical past!

Colne Engaine ༄

The village on the northern slopes of the Colne valley encompassing the lands of five manors, derived its name from Vitales de Ingaine – lord of the manor in 1219.

Over the years a number of personalities have been resident in the village. Miss M. Courtauld, a member of the family now a by-word for their textile empire, turned her thoughts to agriculture and estate management. In 1877, she took over Knights Farm and built up an estate of about 2,000 acres. The work force was controlled by a foreman who took his orders direct from Miss Courtauld. All other matters of management she made her personal responsibility. These included the buying and selling of stock, supervision of buildings and machinery and the overseeing of all routine work. During her years of management, she started what was probably the first Agricultural Training School in the country, with six young women.

She was a great benefactor to the village, donating the present village hall, providing generously to the repairs of the church tower, and well ahead of her time, she devised a method of supplying piped water to dwellings in the main village by the use of hydraulic rams and storage tanks. She was the founder member of the village WI and served for many years on the Parish and Church Councils, also the school management committee. She died in 1935.

During the years of Miss Courtauld's life, the village was not without incident. One resident left his wife one morning announcing that he was going out to kill a cockerel. He did just that. A neighbour named Cockerell lost his head, severed by a scythe. Murder most 'foul' had been committed.

Cranham 🦚

Looking at modern 'Cranham Broadway', it is, perhaps, difficult not to regret the passing of a true village atmosphere. The shops, cars, a modern Plough Inn (which replaced a tiny village pub of the same name) and the assembly yard where District Line trains 'spend the night', all contribute very much to a late 20th century surburban environment.

However, walk a little way to the south of the railway, and you will find green fields and a hill crowned by All Saints church.

Craohu (which became Cranham) was mentioned in the Domesday Book of 1086. It had been held by a Saxon, Alwin, before being given to Odo of Bayeux and held for him, by a man named Hugh.

The first reference to a church in Cranham occurs in 1254, and the building raised in the 13th century lasted until 1873 when the present church was built, at a time when the living was in the gift of St John's College, Oxford. Former fellows of that college were appointed rector.

Cranham Hall has certainly stood near the church since 1600, and perhaps before that. The best known person to reside there was General James Oglethorpe who, in 1743, married Elizabeth Wright, heiress to Cranham Hall. He had returned from two expeditions during which he founded the colony of Georgia, and then defended it against attack from Spain. After his marriage he became a Member of Parliament in 1754 and then retired to farm his wife's estate and to entertain friends like Oliver Goldsmith and Dr Samuel Johnson. He died in 1785, at the great age, for those days, of 89, and is buried in the family vault in All Saints church. Americans still visit the church to lay wreaths on the grave of the founder of Georgia, and they are entertained by local people.

From 1818 to 1854, Cranham's children were taught, at the parish's expense, in the schoolmistress' cottage. A wooden building was then erected for them, and was also used for a Sunday school and for evening classes. The first purpose-built school was erected in 1870 as a memorial to Sarah Boyd, a schoolmistress who had done much for education in the village. She remained in control of the hundred or so children until she retired in 1889, aged 88! 'The Old Boyd School' and the teacher's house still stand, though they have not been used for education since 1950. Cranham has now two primary schools and a large comprehensive school.

Between the 11th and 18th centuries the population of this village stayed at around 200. By 1931 it had passed 1200, and in the next 20 years rose to just under 5000. By 1961 that figure had increased three-fold! Now it becomes important that the Green Belt is not breached further, and that what remains of village life can survive.

Creeksea ༀ

Creeksea is a small village, about three miles from Burnham-on-Crouch. The few houses are reached by one country lane.

At the top of the lane is Creeksea church, originally built in Roman times. It has been rebuilt on the original foundations three times over the years but still retains some of the Roman stone and brickwork. Next to it is Creeksea Hall, the oldest building in Creeksea dating back to the 13th century. Part of the building was demolished and added to, but part of the original building is still standing.

Further down the lane is Creeksea Place, an Elizabethan mansion house built in 1563. Two of the three original wings were demolished in 1741 and a new east wing built on. Adjoining the main house is a bailiff's cottage and a lodge at the main entrance. It stands in extensive grounds. Entrance to the house from Creeksea Lane is through wrought iron gates and over a bridge spanning three ornamental lakes.

The house has always been haunted. Various occupants have all experienced strange happenings, including the ghost of a spirited white stallion. This horse has been seen thundering about the grounds with tail and mane flying. It is said, that a once owner of Creeksea Place was thrown by this horse breaking his neck and the horse was subsequently destroyed, but his ghost lingers on. The house remained unoccupied after the end of the Second World War, after which time it was bought by the present owner in 1950 as a caravan park. The once beautiful grounds are now occupied by about 100 caravans and the house still unused is rapidly falling into decay.

'The Old Tudor Cottage' stands facing the Crouch. A picturesque half timbered black and white building, it was built in 1490 and then known as the Ferry House. The owners had the ferry rights for conveying passengers and cattle across the river to Wallasea Island.

In 1865 the house became the Greyhound Inn. The licencee was a man named Woolf who was renowned for selling the finest brandy in the district. In 1929 extensive restoration work was carried out and a smuggler's den was found. The only access to it was by iron rungs up the old Tudor chimney. Old folks living nearby and who remember it as an inn, immediately said 'That must be where old Woolf hid his brandy'.

Brandy Hole higher up the river is so named as it was a well known spot for the smugglers to dump their brandy, to be recovered later when the coast was clear.

Danbury ✺

Many villages can boast a great house, hall or castle, but Danbury has a palace set in a wooded park, where three peaceful lakes, created in the 13th century, now give pleasure to thousands of visitors in all seasons.

No Royal connections gave the house its status of palace, but great Essex families, St Cleres and D'Arcys, rode and hunted through the deer park from the time that Danbury and its manors were given to Geoffrey de Mandeville, the first Earl of Essex, by William the Conqueror.

Sir Walter Mildmay, founder of Emmanuel College, Cambridge, built a house in the deer park between 1560 and 1589, and called it Danbury Place. The grounds were 'well grown with timber of oaks'. Danbury Place was sold to the Ecclesiastical Commissioners for £24,700, as a residence for George Murray, 96th Bishop of Rochester and it became in 1845, Danbury Palace.

The palace now looked outward to the village. The school children enjoyed annual treats in the park and were rowed round the largest lake by young Mr Murray, the Bishop's son, 'the one who sang the best having the longest ride'. Thus began an association between palace and local people which has continued and extended till the present day. The 98th Bishop, Dr Claughton, entertained the parish to a 'capital supper' for Queen Victoria's Golden Jubilee in 1887, but when he became the 1st Bishop of St Albans the palace ceased to be the official residence of the bishops.

Around the turn of the century Hugh Hoare changed the character of the park when he had 429 oaks cut down. Some local people still remember General and Mrs Wigan, who came to the palace in 1919 and were the last private owners.

In 1947 the park was bought by Essex County Council and a new era began. As late as the 1950s massed daffodils beside the lakes were a glorious sight each spring. The lake area is now a Country Park, attractive and well tended, but there are footpaths where the daffodils once grew. Since then rescue vehicles, ambulances and fire appliances have clattered along the drive with volunteers taking part in Civil Defence exercises, when the palace was the County Civil Defence Headquarters.

From small beginnings in 1969 as a Department of the Mid-Essex Technical College, a prestigious Management Centre has evolved. A new residential unit was opened by Sir John Ruggles Brise in 1974 and the Danbury Park Management Centre in its present form was officially opened in October 1985. Danbury Park School, in its own corner, was opened in 1974 chiefly to accommodate children from the new housing developments nearby, and is a thriving and active part of village life.

Dedham

Dedham lies in 'Constable country' on the border of Essex and Suffolk between Colchester and Ipswich. It is bordered on the north side by the river Stour which forms the boundary between the two counties. John Constable, the famous landscape painter,

Dedham Vale

lived at Flatford, two and a half miles down river from Dedham, but he was educated at the old grammar school in Dedham, and found inspiration for many of his paintings from the local countryside. The grammar school was founded in 1571 and four years later was granted a charter by Queen Elizabeth I. It is a handsome building which has been added to over the years and is now divided into two private houses.

During the 13th and 14th centuries the village became prosperous through the weaving industry, and the magnificent church, which dominates the village, was built at this time, largely through the generosity of two leading wool merchants. It is well known in the area for its wonderful flower arrangements, particularly at Harvest Festival time. Since 1965 most of the old pews have been replaced by new ones, individually carved in memory of parishioners or some historical event such as man's first landing on the moon.

Dedham is rich in architecture, from the medieval Flemish cottages to the elegant houses of the High Street with their Tudor framework and Georgian facades. One of these, built originally as a clothier's house, was owned by the Sherman family, ancestors of General Sherman of the American Civil War. It is now owned by the National Trust. The Flemish cottages are Tudor cottages built to form a quadrangle round the master weaver's house, and were homes for the Flemish weavers brought in to teach the locals the art of weaving.

The river has played a large part in the history of Dedham, and until recently there was a large working corn mill, painted by Constable, and now converted into luxury flats. There is still a thriving boat hire business, and the water meadows make a popular picnic place in the summer. In earlier days the river provided facilities for washing the cloth woven in the district as well as providing water for both humans and animals. It also served as a highway for the transport of goods to and from the market towns along its banks. Le Talbooth, now a well-known restaurant, was originally the toll station for boats using the river, but it fell into ruin and at one time was used as a lime kiln.

Farming has always been an important side of Dedham life, and although the dairy farms are now gone, sheep have returned in large numbers. At one time the village had eight smithies of which Forge Street is now the only reminder. Footpaths are a legacy of the old farming days, and are kept in good condition by the parish council in conjunction with a local footpath society. One of these paths carries the curious name of Pennypots. At one time it led to the site of a pest house on the outer edge of the village and its name derives from the custom of leaving money in a jar at the village boundary in exchange for provisions brought by outsiders in times of plague. Near this footpath lies a small plot of land known as The Cage. This marks the site of the old village lock-up.

Today, tourism could be said to be Dedham's chief industry. People come from all over the world to see the site of some of Constable's best known paintings and to visit the house and studio of another later artist, Sir Alfred Munnings.

Tourism brings its own problems, and the parish council and local preservation society work hard to keep the village unspoilt and yet a viable place in which to live. Great care has been taken to preserve the beauty and dignity of the High Street, and yet at the same time there are excellent shopping facilities, which include a butcher, a chemist, and an excellent grocer and delicatessen.

Downham ✒

Lying between Wickford and Billericay the small village of Downham is a pleasing mixture of period cottages, farmhouses and newer properties mostly built in keeping with the rural atmosphere.

Clustered together are the village pond, the small roadside garden created to commemorate Queen Elizabeth II's Silver Jubilee, the old school now converted into a house and the village hall.

Approaching the village from Wickford, St Margaret's church dominates the skyline. A church has stood on this site since and possibly before the 11th century. Various restorations and rebuildings have occurred over the centuries, the last being as recently as 1977 when a 16 year old boy deliberately set fire to the church by pouring oil on the altar and lighting it. Fortunately the Tudor tower and the outer stone walls were saved, but the roof, interior and beautiful stained glass windows were utterly destroyed. The church has now been completely restored, the villagers who refused to let their church die raised £25,000 towards the rebuilding costs.

Below the church lies Downham Hall, now smaller than the original 17th century mansion, at one time the home of the De Beauvoir family, descendants of Osmund De Beauvoir who was rector of Downham for 60 years and whose name is immortalised in the De Beauvoir Arms, the village public house.

An original 17th century dovecote still stands in the vicinity of Downham Hall and there is evidence of Roman remains around the hall and the church, giving rise to the belief that an early Saxon settlement existed there.

Two other interesting older houses in the village are Downham House, originally the home of a branch of the well known Gascoyne-Cecil family and the Grange which up until the late 1960s was owned by the Keddie family who tragically lost all three of their sons in the Second World War. Two of the bells in the church were recast at their expense and dedicated to the memory of their sons.

The old pump which once supplied the whole village with water still stands on the hill, below the inn, restored and maintained by the Parish Council.

The northern boundary takes in part of the attractive South Hanningfield reservoir, a favourite haunt of bird watchers hoping for a glimpse of rare waterfowl: but the deep dark waters have their own secret, for beneath them lies the once grand manor house of Fremnells and concealed within its murky walls is a mysterious room with a ramp believed to have been a hiding place used by the notorious highwayman Dick Turpin and his famous horse, Black Bess. When the flooding of the land was completed the Water Company built a largish house as a residence for the manager of the reservoir and named it Fremnells in memory of its historic predecessor.

Duddenhoe End 🐚

The picturesque little hamlet of Duddenhoe End with its share of old world thatched cottages sits in the north-west corner of Essex, on the top of the 'Champion', a hill of the East Anglian Heights about 410 feet above sea level with an ancient history.

Local clay was used for making the black dye used by the Anglo-Flemish wool trade. One merchant was William Cade (died 1166) of East Anglia who probably used the old Roman road once called Cades Lane before becoming Beards Lane. Another use of this clay was in the manufacturing of clay pipes.

Duddas Hall was held by the Saxon Dudda, Earl of Wessex in 1066, after which the first Norman name appears and the name changed to Duddenhoe Grange and was placed into the hands of Abbots of Tilty Abbey. After Henry VIII demolished the monasteries it became the property of the Earls of Suffolk, then Lord Audley de Walden as part of the Audley End estates.

The green was known as Bridge Green and is still recognized on ordnance survey maps today, taking its name from 'the Champion' Thomas le Bruges 1273 and held by John le Bruggere in 1294. This Norman family named the hill, Champion.

During the 17th century 'the green' became Duddenhoe End with thatch cottages dotting both sides of the road. This took in most of 'the green' leaving a small part at the west end and this became the recreation place for the village where fêtes, teas and fairs were held. The most frequent visitor was the Langley Brass Band, playing most Sunday mornings. These people were dissidents from the Anglican church and a little cottage was converted into a Methodist chapel with about 80 members, but closed down in 1935.

Timber was a big industry for the estate, having approximately 450 acres of woodland in 1808. These woods were familiar to the hunt back to when the countryside was open fields. Since 1725 the Puckridge Hunt hunted over these lands and Rockells Wood was known as 'the joy of fox hunters'.

The Wilkes family of Lofts Hall, Wenden Lofts had purchased most of the area by 1866. The Rev Robert Fiske (Wilkes) acting as squire controlled the life of the community, from the 10th century church dedicated to St Dunstan with which Duddenhoe End was associated until its closure in 1928. In 1859 the barn of its glebe farm 'The Parsonage' was converted into 'Hamlet Church'. This beautiful little church is reputed to be the only thatched church in Essex and is well worth a visit.

East Hanningfield 🌿

The main road of the village, is largely unchanged in outline, since John Walker made maps of the area in the 17th century.

The church of All Saints, which was very ancient, was destroyed by fire as the result of a faulty flue pipe, in December 1883. A medieval painting was removed from the old church and is now housed in the Victoria and Albert Museum. This building dated from about 1381 and until the plague, was the centre of the village. A stream, called the Pan, runs nearby, also 'Frogs Island' the watery site of osier beds which provided a village basket making industry.

The new church consecrated in 1885, stands in the present village, on the Tye. There are three old public houses, The Horseshoes 1720, The Windmill 1662 and the Plough and Sail 1704. The shop which is also the post office has a Dutch roof and boasts a Queen Victoria pillar box. Nearby stood the forge, a scene of much industry earlier this century.

The old rectory, now a block of luxury flats, was set in spacious grounds, with many beautiful trees and an attractive stable block. Near the kitchen door was a well sunk in 1790. It was 347 feet deep and was built of 39,500 bricks, without the aid of cement. This well was one of the deepest in the country, providing water free for villagers who came before 10 am. A pump for public use stood on the green. This was fenced around with white railings, and until the mains water supply, frequently used.

The manor stands away from the village, has been restored and is now a lovely residence. Several old houses remain in East Hanningfield – Willis Farm, Rails Farmhouse, Huntingdons, Paprills, Common Farm, Salesfrith Farm and The Hall are all examples of the village heritage.

Cattle and arable farming have been the chief method of making a livelihood, but now an industrial estate is in operation, also chicken breeding farms and hatcheries. An old mill is still standing in the village where corn was ground.

In 1863 a Church school was opened, but prior to this a bungalow was used as a dame school. This Church school is now a private house. The village now has a new primary school and community centre.

Several local characters lie buried in the churchyard in unmarked graves. 'Friday' Lord the chimney sweep was to be seen riding a bike, with his brushes and rods tied to the crossbar. He and his clothes were so covered with soot that only the whites of his eyes gleamed. 'Poddy' Reeve the blacksmith toiled in his forge, wrapped in a leather apron. The gnarled old men who had retired gathered in his 'shop' for a gossip daily. Mr Wood the cobbler lived in a small room surrounded by brads and fat tabby cats. Mr and Mrs Wood were very short and stout, ideally matched in fact. Mr Wood managed to hold a conversation with a mouth full of small nails.

The Eastons & Tilty

Little Easton was also known as 'Estaines Parva', meaning small, or 'Easton by the Manor' as the residence of the lord was here from the 12th century.

There is no lord now but many 'Bakers' and 'Barkers' still living in the village, descended from the men who barked the trees, as charcoal burning was a local occupation. 'Butcher' is a local name coming from 'Bouchier' the name of the old lords of Estaines in 1420. An interesting thing to note is the letter 'M' on several old houses in the village which came from the name Maynard, a man who was granted the manor of Easton and all its entitlements by Queen Elizabeth I.

Frances Evelyn Maynard inherited the estate of Easton Lodge in 1865 at the age of three. She became the Countess of Warwick in 1893, when her husband succeeded to the title.

H. G. Wells was a writing friend of the Countess of Warwick and came to live at The Glebe, the old parsonage in 1911. This home saw the comings and goings of distinguished people in the world of literature and the arts. While at The Glebe, H. G. Wells wrote *Mr Britling Sees It Through* a semi-autobiographical novel based on Little Easton during the First World War.

Amateur theatricals were a constant diversion for the Wells family and their guests, and these could often be performed at the Barn Theatre, the great tithe barn beside the church, which the Countess of Warwick turned into a theatre at the turn of the century. The Countess's dear friend Ellen Terry performed many times at the Barn. Shaw produced *The Taming of the Shrew* and Ellen Terry coached the cast. There is a plaque in memory of Ellen Terry in Little Easton church.

The 'Fighting Parson of Great Easton', the Reverend Horatio Bladen Capel, was born at Easton Lodge, which was his home until he came to Great Easton in 1877. Having been a champion boxer in the Navy in the days of sail, he was to encounter much opposition, as he was a dictator practicing high church worship, and Great Easton was very low church. His chief opponent was the village blacksmith. Much discussion and argument took place between them and finally the rector said to the blacksmith 'Let's fight it out and the best man will be the winner'. So into the churchyard they both went, the rector won and from then on they were the best of friends.

Tilty was well established in the 12th century, with its abbey of St Mary the Virgin, arable and grazing land, fish ponds and vineyards. However, much of the abbey and buildings were destroyed by the soldiers of King John through a dispute with the Prior over extortionate taxes in the early 1200s.

There remains of this extensive abbey just the chapel at the gate, now the parish church for Tilty and Duton Hill, with its beautifully restored east window and a section of the old flint wall on an adjoining meadow.

It was the Reverend Hugh Cuthbertson, vicar of Tilty, who having had experience of curing tobacco in South America started the tobacco plant club in about 1949. This is now carried on by his daughter Mrs Cecily Down at 'Abbey Gates', the former vicarage. Plants are supplied to members early in the year, and these are sent back to her for curing in the special kilns in the autumn. Club membership is now nationwide.

Epping ✑

Epping is situated on the highest point in Essex – its High Street is at the same level as the cross on the top of St Paul's Cathedral. It has a flourishing market and specialist shops which encourage visitors from all around the area.

Separated from the great metropolis of London by a beautiful and extensive forest some 7 miles long, there were as many as 16 taverns and inns in the High Street because travellers made Epping their last staging post in the days when highwaymen, including Dick Turpin, robbed the wealthy. Rather than travel through the forest after dark, the stage coaches and their passengers would spend the night in Epping before proceeding to London.

Epping has been renowned through the centuries for butter and cream and its sausages are still being made and have achieved international fame.

Camille Pissarro (1830 – 1903) the famous French impressionist stayed with his son Lucien in Hemnall Street and painted many scenes of Epping. The house has a plaque to commemorate the fact. There is also a plaque in Buttercross Lane at the home of one of the world's leading naturalists and lepidopterists, Henry Doubleday.

Sir Winston Churchill is another famous person connected with Epping. He lived for 4 years in Wood House, a mansion where Rod Stewart now resides, on the Copped Hall estate. Copped Hall is a ruin as it has never been restored since it was burnt out in 1917. It is about a mile to the south of Epping. This beautifully proportioned historic building can boast the footsteps of Henry VIII, Mary Tudor, Queen Elizabeth I and it is claimed that Shakespeare's *A Midsummer Night's Dream* was first performed in Copped Hall's famous Italian garden.

Hill Hall, to the east of Epping, is another well-known old house. It is described as one of the most important Elizabethan mansions in England with its unique 16th century wall paintings.

On Mondays, which are the market days, colourful stalls are erected along one side of the High Street. Cattle and sheep were sold there until foot and mouth disease made it impracticable shortly after the Second World War. In 1833 a man sold his wife for 2/6d and got himself drunk on the proceeds.

Epping would have been severed from its famous forest when the M25 motorway was constructed had it not been for the protests of local inhabitants. A cricket pitch stood on the proposed route. Just after the Second World War the ground had been flattened and made playable by sheer hard work. When it was threatened by the motorway there was such an outcry that it was decided that a tunnel should be built. This involved cutting away a wide stretch of land to the depth of the tunnel. After the tunnel had been completed and covered with earth the cricket field had to be restored. Now the players boast that they play on the most expensive pitch in the world – it cost more than £10 million.

Feering

By-passed by the A12 for over 20 years, the village of Feering has been said to derive its Saxon name from Feringe, or 'dwellers by the road'. The old Roman road to Colchester passed through Feering.

The centre of the old village of Feering lies to the north of the Roman road. On the rising ground above the flood plain of the

Blackwater lies the village green. Its post office and general store and old cottages, one with a dovecote, are overlooked by the square tower of the village church. The newer buildings on two sides of the green remind the observer of the building which has occured in the village this century, but the church has dominated the story of Feering.

The parish once belonged to Edward the Confessor, last of the Saxon kings, and was exchanged by William the Conqueror for Old Windsor with the Abbot of Westminster, who became rector of Feering. The responsibilities of the Abbots of Westminster, as rectors, for the maintenance of the chancel of the church have in recent times, devolved on the Church Commissioners of England.

A visitor to All Saints church enters through a beautiful Tudor brick porch which has been carefully restored. The porch was the gift of a 15th century wool merchant, and his mark is in the porch roof. Like many old churches, the building has been added to over several centuries from the 13th century nave to the 15th century tower with its eight bells. It has been lovingly repaired and cared for since, often by East Anglian craftsmen, although the present chancel arch was designed by Sir George Gilbert Scott, as a young man, in 1845.

Not far from the church, on the old glebeland, stands Feering village school, opened in 1842 and in use until 1987. It is perhaps a measure of the comparative importance of education and cultivation in 19th century Feering, that the first head teacher in 1842 was the vicar's gardener.

The village inn, appropriately named the Bell, has stood near the church for many centuries, facing the village green and the old almshouses, now converted into cottages. These 10 almshouses were sold to their occupants by the vicar for £300 in 1938 when the rental was not worth the cost of collection! Next to these cottages lies Church Farm, a reminder of the days when every church had its own means of support from the land around it and of Feering's dependence on agriculture until recent times.

Within the parish of Feering are many small communities of a few houses, all part of the larger village community. A new bungalow at Stocks green is the only reminder of where the stocks once stood, but Feeringbury has been the manor house since the Abbots of Westminster used to enjoy staying there.

A regular visitor to Feering was the painter John Constable. It is

54

appropriate that the altar piece of the Risen Christ painted by him in 1822 for the chapel at Manningtree hangs over the altar in the lady chapel of Feering parish church. This picture and a painting of Feering vicarage were included in the 1976 Tate Gallery exhibition of Constable's work.

Felsted ✤

The Felsted WI banner has as its emblem, a barrel wreathed by circling fish – a motif better suited to a fishing port than a village in the heart of arable Essex, one might think . . . unless one knows the history of the so-called 'herring window' inside the wagon arch linking the street to the parish church.

Lord Riche, in residence at Leez Priory, endowed a chantry at Felsted in 1555, following the custom of wealthy men, by making some provision for the local poor (and a kind of spiritual insurance for himself, through the regular prayers to be chanted by its chaplain for the benefactor!). The revenue from certain parcels of land was to be used by the churchwardens, to provide 11 barrels of white herrings and 11 barrels of red herrings (ie kippers) for distribution on Ash Wednesdays and a further 7 barrels of each on every Lenten Sunday. Incidentally, 20 of each fish were to be kept for the chaplain's own use, and the wardens were bidden to keep all the barrels! This custom continued (at Little Leez and Much Waltham too) until 1851, when a more realistic gift of cash was substituted.

The 'herring window' can still be seen under the arch of what was the Guildhall (before it became the original school room.) One of the signatories of the chantry's founding document was a George Boote, churchwarden and builder, whose son followed him in the trade and built 2 remarkable houses in the village. One, on the corner facing the 'herring window', is inscribed 'Geo. Boote built this house 1596' and some say that the figurine on its wall comes to life and wanders the street on Hallowe'en.

Oliver Cromwell married a local girl! His wife, Elizabeth, was daughter to Sir John Bourchier, who rented a farm, Grandcourts, near French's Green, from Lord Warwick.

Fiddlers Hamlet 🎻

Fiddlers Hamlet lies 1½ miles south-west of Epping, in the parish of Theydon Garnon, which itself was once a hamlet of Epping. The hamlet is still surrounded by farmland, but this charming old English scene has had to be carved up for motorways. The beauty of the countryside can still be admired, but the sounds of animals and birds are no longer all that can be heard. Fiddlers Hamlet has been a centre of population since the 17th century but now comprises a dozen houses or so.

Stand at the crossroads, facing towards Epping, and on your right you will see the picturesque Home Farm and farm buildings some 400 years old, with the gnarled old trees guarding the entrance.

The Merry Fiddlers Inn is another 400 year building, but which has had a few additions built on to it. This is where the hamlet got its name. Walk past the inn, over the bridge. The medieval house on your left is Masons Bridge Farm and is the oldest building in the hamlet although it does not look it from the outside, having a modern exterior. Over 50 years ago this farm stabled race horses and there was a track here where racing took place. Later, a nine hole golf course was laid and Bridge Farm became the club house. Nowadays it is a private dwelling and the land belongs to another farmer.

Retrace your footsteps over the bridge and stop at the houses opposite the inn. It was here that an annual fair was held, but in 1872 Chisenhale Marsh, the lord of the manor, abolished it by petition. This is probably the spot where the fiddlers came and played. There was a cobbler's shop and a grocer on the corner, although many traders called and travelled round the neighbourhood. During the Second World War a Nissen hut was erected in which to hold church services and social evenings but it was later demolished. Theydon Garnon's 700 year old church lies some 2 miles away and until recent times parishioners always walked over the fields to attend.

Turn left and take the road to Coopersale but as you walk past Home Farm look ahead and on the right you will vaguely see the old school and the bells which rang out to summon the children to school.

If you glance to the right you will see a magnificent building on the hill – Gaynes Park, with a long curving drive with parkland on both sides. This was the home of the Chisenhale Marshes which they vacated in 1976. Happily the family, or part of it, live in Theydon Mount and still farm the land. In the past the Chisenhale Marshes, who have lived in this district since the 1800s and who have manorial rights, held garden parties and open days when the people of Theydon Garnon and Coopersale enjoyed themselves in the grounds, sat in the attractive gardens and looked around the farm itself.

Finchingfield 🌿

When the Festival of Britain was being organised in 1951 it was decided by the London committee that it would be a delightful attraction to select four or five of the prettiest villages in Britain and present them to the visitors as examples of true England. Finchingfield was one of the chosen. Visitors came to the Festival and many of them found their way or were brought by officials to admire. The Festival ended but the fame the occasion brought to the village did not fade. Calendars, postcards, tapestries, paintings and crafts, all depicting the loveliness of an Essex village kept Finchingfield very near the top of the tourists' itinerary.

On the east side of the pond adjacent to the hand bridge is the old workhouse. In 1767 there were 30 inmates. Several years ago the old workhouse was a butcher's shop and today is a delightful private residence.

Past the workhouse and on up the hill, to the Green Man and the Guildhall, now 450 years of age. In 1630 a school for poor children was formed by the generosity of Sir Robert Kempe. Under his will the Guildhall and the adjoining almshouses were then given to the poor of the parish. Today the Guildhall is used for exhibitions, committee meetings, lectures and the occasional social evening. It is an integral part of the life of the village as it has been for over 400 years.

The tiny museum facing the entrance to the Guildhall tells much of the hard work done by the labourers, the craftsmen and the straw plaiters.

In her book about village life and characters Eliza Vaughan,

The Green at Finchinfield

whose father was installed as vicar in 1864, tells the story of a
woman who died. The corpse lay in the coffin downstairs and the
relatives were upstairs sorting out the possessions of the departed.
They found a box containing some strange little things that looked
useless but which they suspected of being imps, so they burned
them. When they went down to look once more on the earthly
remains of someone who had been suspected of witchcraft they
found only a heap of ashes.

When one resident came to Finchingfield he began to repair his
cottage and embedded in the walls was a stick. It had obviously
been put there for some purpose and he investigated. The experts
came from London and verified that it was a witch stick. It is a
slim stave with a serpent carved at the head in an anti-clockwise
twist. It was not as it was first thought to be a tool for black magic,
but quite the opposite. It was embedded in the plaster to ward off
evil intentions and to divert the malicious glance of any witch who
might be passing that way.

If there are doubts about witches there is no doubt about the
beauty of St John the Baptist church which stands on top of the hill
and seems to be a symbol of strength and security. It is over 400
years old and has withstood religious wars, political machinations
and gale force winds. Once a year this lovely old church is the
scene of a Flower Festival.

If it should be thought that Finchingfield is sunk in the past then
the thought is far from the truth. The number of clubs and
interests is wide and varied. The Wiffen Coaches for instance are
the epitome of modern luxury. It is difficult to believe that before
1913 the only transport in and out of the village was by horse
drawn vehicles.

Fingringhoe 🌿

Unlike many English villages, Fingringhoe does not nestle, but spreads, east and west, along a rise overlooking the beautiful Roman river valley. Travelling five miles south from Colchester, the country road climbs gently to cross the bridge over the narrow tidal river, then springs up to the centre where all the facilities necessary for a true village are gathered round Church Green.

The pond, fed from a spring, is home to a colony of mallards and kingfishers have been seen, diving from bordering trees. The splendid oaktree, in the middle of the steeply sloping green, is said to have grown from an acorn buried with someone long ago, a smuggler perhaps, for smugglers have a place in the story of Fingringhoe.

Village people have worshipped for 900 years in St Andrew's church, built in 1100 and enlarged in the 14th and 15th centuries. It is peaceful, welcoming and bright with white plastered walls, fading medieval wall paintings and homely faces of 14th century local people carved on the timbers of the unusual barrel roof. Smugglers were rumoured to hide their contraband behind the battlements.

Stories of smuggling are easy to believe for the farmland slopes south down to eerie marshes through which curves Geedon Creek, often covered in drifting mists and silent except for the calls of shoreline birds. Here once was South Green, one of the three greens around which the population clustered. A census of 1881 listed many cottages whose occupants were agricultural labourers, with one shepherd who spent his life caring for the sheep grazing on the borders of the marshes. Sheep still graze there but sadly the people have gone and their cottages have long since fallen down. The Green has disappeared under the plough but some of the cottages were saved and have been restored and converted for modern living, keeping the name as a reminder of the people who have gone before.

On the west side of Church Green is another important amenity of any village, the ancient inn, in this case called The Whalebone which, until quite recently displayed the decaying jawbones of the great sea creature as its sign, perhaps brought by a returning sailor to one of the nearby quays at Rowhedge or across the river Colne at Wivenhoe. Two old cottages remain and share with the inn a most beautiful view over the Roman river valley. Church Green has only one old cottage left but recently new cottages have been built opposite especially for older residents. This scheme was made possible by gifts of land and money and the hard work of the Church Green Trust who have made this great contribution to village life.

Built in 1887 the Church school shares the Green. It is a happy school with an active Parent Teacher Association. Modern amenities include the post office, a village shop and the village hall where the Women's Institute and a Friendship Club for older residents meet. The Methodist church close by has an active membership.

The manor has been held by different families but reverted to the Crown until Edward VI granted it to the Darcy family in 1553, who lived here for nearly 100 years and rebuilt Fingringhoe Hall in the early 17th century. Sadly the main wing of the house was destroyed in a fire recently.

Fire has brought destruction once before this century when part of the mill built in Tudor times was destroyed. Rebuilt, it still functions, though tidal power has given way to oil and the tall brown barge sails are no longer to be seen on the mill pond.

The Nature Reserve at Fingringhoe Wick attracts many visitors. Quarrying last century left deep holes, now lakes, which attract herons and a variety of water fowl. Nightingales have returned and geese winter on the marshes.

Fobbing ❧

Fobbing lays quietly overlooking the marshes, with Basildon to the north and the river Thames to the south, at the head of a tributary of Hole Haven Creek. Its history goes back into the mists of time with smugglers and a well documented revolt among its local peasants in 1381.

The church tower can be seen from many vantage points around the area. One Tree Hill, a local beauty spot is the highest point (in a direct line) before the North Pole, with Westley Heights being on the same ridge of hills overlooking the Thames. West Lee was the name of the manorial estate once owned by the Bishop of London and it was against this system and heavy taxes that the peasants led by Wat Tyler and Jack Straw revolted. A local resident Thomas Baker is reputed to have struck the first blow by killing the King's tax collector at Brentwood.

Until 1953 and the east coast floods the creek from Fobbing was navigable to the sea. With a little imagination on a misty day it is easy to see the smugglers bringing in their contraband of 'brandy for the parson and 'baccy for the clerk'. It was supposed the clergy were involved and the fact the old rectory has such large cellars seems to lend credence to this idea.

The Dukes Head (Fobbing Road) is thought by many to have been a public house. Although built for that purpose, a licence did not become available in the area and it was run for many years by the Wood family as an off licence. The teenagers would congregate there and the local police requested Mr Wood's father to keep them in check; he encouraged them by forming a football team and cricket club.

On a derelict farm near the Five Bells stands an old bungalow now used as a cow-shed. Many years ago a Mr Cash lived here and it was he who started up the Vange Water Company. The company bottled water from the well between One Tree Hill and Hovells Farm. The Temple Well has been visited by many locals and their relatives. It died out after about 5 or 6 years but by then Mr Cash had made his money. The bottles were 2/6d each and people came down from London to collect their supplies. Whether it cured them or not was questionable. Towards the end of the active life of the Vange Water Company there was a dispute with a Mr Poole at Hovells Farm. He stopped the flow of water to the Vange well by digging one for himself and bottling his own brand for a short spell.

Fobbing wharf ruins can still be seen today and the tide used to come up the creek to the brickworks. The Kynocks Ammunitions Factory was down on the marshes (now the site of the Mobil Oil Refinery) and people who worked there were commuters on the Corringham Light Railway. There was a colony for workers in the region of the Mobil Pegasus Club.

Frinton ✧

Frinton got its name from a Saxon warrior. In Anglo Saxon the settlement where he landed was known as Fritha's tun meaning Fritha's farm.

Still standing today is the old parish church of St Mary, the smallest complete church in Essex. Parts of the nave are of Norman origin. The first recorded rector was appointed in 1199. The old church remains open for services and for the daily use of all who seek a quiet place for prayer and meditation.

Many coastal communities resorted to smuggling and Frinton was no exception. The old church was a stowage place for vessels at first. There used to be a cloth hung across the church to part half of it for a smuggler's warehouse. The smuggled goods were removed inland by horses taken from any farm near the coast. The contraband business finally died out in 1867.

Medieval Frinton was similar to many other agricultural villages but it differed from most in its small size both in area and population. In the 1230s its total extent was probably not more than 600 acres.

It was not until the latter part of the 19th century that Frinton achieved any significance in the world at large and then only by a complete revolution to turn it into a high class watering place. In 1886 some roads were laid out, the railway came in 1887. For 10 years things went very slowly. However by 1901 the population had grown to 645.

With the great boom in golf south of the Scottish border, a golf course was planned along the Greensward and adjacent fields and the first clubhouse was built in 1899. The Frinton Lawn Tennis, Croquet and Bowls Club was formed in 1900. In its third year it held an open tournament and later this was to grow into a tournament of worldwide significance with a number of Wimbledon finalists featuring in the winners list.

The Frinton Summer Theatre, now one of the only repertory companies left in England, uses the Frinton WI hall for six weeks during the summer. Many leading stars today had early experience on the Frinton stage.

Frinton's greatest pride is its Greensward and sea front. The Old Wick Farmhouse still stands in Old Road. It dates back to the 18th century and for many years was the Council House.

Among many famous inhabitants was Ursula Bloom in the First World War. She wrote the book *Rosemary for Frinton*. Gracie Fields' house at the beginning of Connaught Avenue was called 'Tinkerbell' and she used it to give sick and deprived children holidays. Marconi started the first Wireless Telegraph School to teach students how to use his new invention, in No 34 Upper Third Avenue.

Fryerning 🌿

Fryerning is a small village occupying one of the two sandy gravel eminences of central Essex. It lies about 100 feet above its near neighbour Ingatestone, with which it is closely associated. Fryerning has an interesting and beautiful church, three public houses and no shops. There are several spacious houses.

After the Norman Conquest its owner, Gilbert Montfitchet gave the area to the Knights Hospitallers, who built the church tower, and three generations later Sir Nicholas Wadham acquired the manor. He married Dorothy, a daughter of William Petre, and they founded Wadham College, Oxford. The college is still the patron of the church and owns considerable land in the vicinity.

The nave of the small church is of Norman origin, as shown by the thick walls the five small rounded windows high up from the ground and the two rounded Norman doors. Another indication of Norman origin is that the walls are constructed of pudding-stone, hardened concretions of sandstone and pebbles, dark brown with iron and found locally in glacial gravels in Essex. These are reinforced with courses of Roman tiles and quartz pebbles.

None of the glass is of special interest except the recently installed memorial to Airey Neave, murdered by the INLA in the precincts of the House of Commons. He lived in the village as a boy.

Of special interest is the font made of Caen stone and finely carved with ancient symbols. There are similar ones at Little Laver and Abbess Roding.

Mill Green, the northern limb of the village, is pleasantly wooded. Besides its possession of the only public house in the country known to have the name of the Viper, it was once an area producing in the Middle Ages, noted pottery made from its local clay and sold extensively in London. There is still a good deal of evidence of this, especially near Potter Row Farm.

Also at Mill Green are the ruins of the Hyde. This was once the habitation of the Disney family, whose much neglected memorial is to be found in the churchyard. The house was burnt down in 1965, but it was John Disney who gained a reputation as a collector of antiques in the late 18th century and who founded the first Chair of Archaeology at Cambridge.

Another former inhabitant of Fryerning, but in a completely different field, was Daniel Sutton. He was the man who helped to perfect the process of inoculation against smallpox, and who in 1763 established a surgery in Ingatestone, but resided at Fryerning. He attained a good deal of success, though the treatment was later supplanted by vaccination.

Other old houses of note are Adkins and Spilfeathers, both in Back Lane, and Trueloves in the south of the parish, associated with a former ale taster of that name in the 14th century.

Fyfield ⚜

Fyfield is a rural parish situated on the B184, 2½ miles north of Ongar. It is a sprawling village with a population of about 900. It has been called 'the gateway to the Roothings', the series of villages through which the river Roding flows on its way to the Thames. The Roding enters Fyfield from the north-east and leaves the parish in the south-west. Fyfield is also crossed by that ancient footpath, the Essex Way, on its route towards East Anglia. The area is mainly agricultural with high quality soil.

The village boasts its own flower, the Fyfield Pea, *Lathyrus Tuberosus*, thought to have originated in Eastern Europe. Looking rather like a small sweet pea, it is a bushy or climbing perennial 2–3 feet high with crimson, slightly fragrant flowers in June/July. It grows on grassy verges and in the hedgerows of the area, but sadly is now becoming scarce. The local primary school have adopted it as part of their emblem and it will be carved on the village sign.

Nowadays the village has one well stocked general store incorporating the post office, a restaurant and two public houses. The Black Bull on the main Ongar – Dunmow route is about 400 years old. It was once licensed for slaughtering and was also a stage coach and carrier point. The Queen's Head in Queen Street is of similar age and both are welcoming country pubs providing good food and drink.

Education in Fyfield goes back over 300 years, when in 1687 the rector, Dr Anthony Walker, endowed a free school for poor children. A transcript of part of his will can be seen on a wooden plaque on the west wall of the church. The present school, a modern building, still bears his name – Dr Walker's Church of England Primary School.

St Nicholas' church, which is of an unusual design with a central tower, is of Norman origin with the north and south aisles added in the 13th century. It is built of rubble and clunch with cement rendering, but this slightly drab exterior belies some distinctive features inside. Visitors should especially note the fine 14th century sedilia, stepped in three bays, set into the wall on the south side of the sanctuary, surmounted by three balls, the symbols of St Nicholas, patron saint of pawnbrokers.

It is recorded that the headless body of Henry, Lord Scrope of Masham, whose family were patrons of the church in the 12th century, is buried under the organ in the north side of the choir chancel. Henry V suspected him of being a traitor and he was beheaded at Portchester Castle, but after Agincourt he was pardoned and his headless body was returned to Fyfield.

The watermill, also mentioned in the Domesday Book, can be seen from the bridge over the river Roding, making a picturesque part of a private dwelling. Fyfield once had a windmill too, but this was blown down in a gale in 1910, though its site can still be clearly identified.

There are an unusual number of timber framed houses, some moated, in Fyfield, all privately owned and not open to the public. Fyfield Hall, the manor house, contains a rare aisled hall and trussed rafter roof. Also timber framed is the moated medieval manor house of Lampetts. Both now produce wine from their own vineyards.

Galleywood 🐚

Although in Saxon times a settlement probably existed in Galleywood, down the years it was no more than a hamlet of Great Baddow. With the building of the fine parish church on the common, it was granted the status of an ecclesiastical parish in 1874. Not until 1987 did it become a civil parish, separate from Baddow, and administered by its own Parish Council. The name Gavelwode appears in 1250, probably deriving from the Saxon 'gavol', or rent, paid for the woods around the settlement.

Perhaps the village's main claim to fame is its historic racecourse, and it can safely be said that it is the only racecourse in the country which encircles the village church, dating back to the 18th century.

In 1890 a new racecourse with a new grandstand was formed. It twice crossed the main road, which was covered with tan made from oak bark, and all traffic was stopped during the races. Flat racing gave place to steeplechasing and the races became a great local occasion. Twice yearly a two-day meeting was held, the first mainly attended by the gentry and the second by farm workers and townspeople. Because of the danger to children from traffic the school was closed on race days.

Steeplechasing at Galleywood came to an end in 1935, as the national economic crisis affected attendances, but the grandstand was not dismantled at that time, and remained to serve as a venue for many village activities, until the generosity of Mrs Keene produced the Keene Hall.

There are many 16th century houses in Galleywood, mainly in Well Lane, where there are three wells. At one time they provided the main water supply, and indeed the piped water supply did not reach the village until 1930. Goat Hall is another 16th century house, while Wild Wood Cottage in Galley End was built in 1640, by one Louis Monsant, in peculiar style: he provided a watertight roof by inverting an old boat on the walls and covered it with pitch. During conversions some years ago the main keel and ribs of the boat were revealed, and barnacles and other shellfish were clearly visible. A similar roof can be seen in The Street.

St Michael and All Angels' church on Galleywood Common owes its existence to 'Squire Pryor' who bought the mansion of

Hylands. He was the wealthy chairman of a brewery, who was persuaded by his deeply religious wife to finance the building of the church at Widford, and also one on the high ground of Galleywood Common, which is still a landmark visible for many miles. Arthur Pryor laid the foundation stone in 1872 and later attended the consecration ceremony in 1873, when bellringers rang 5060 changes on the new bells. If Mrs Pryor cherished any hopes of attending Sunday services at Galleywood with her husband and nine children, they were soon dashed. Mr Pryor disliked the first sermon he heard there, which to him smacked of 'popery', and could not be persuaded to attend another service in the church on which he had spent £6,300.

Goldhanger 🌿

The village lies near the north shore of the tidal estuary of the river Blackwater, some five miles below Maldon and ten miles from the open sea, at the head of a small creek. No watercourse of any kind now flows into the head of the creek, though a stream runs down to the estuary half a mile to the east of the village and another a mile to the west, and on both these streams is the site of an ancient manor house. The creek itself must have been a useful waterway, and up to the early years of the last century fishing smacks unloaded their catch at the quay at the bottom of the road called Fish Street which leads up to the Square.

The parish church of St Peter dates from the 11th century. Considerable rebuilding was carried out in the 14th and 15th centuries and again in the 19th century. There is a fine altar table of the early 18th century.

John Knight obtained a licence in the 17th century to use some of his buildings as a school, and there was a National School by the 1830s. The present school was built next to the tithe barn in Church Street in 1875. There are also memories of a dame school held towards the end of the 19th century in part of the Old Rectory beside the church.

Over the centuries occupations here have included farming, fishing, saltmaking, spinning, milling and, of course, smuggling.

A Thames barge near Goldhanger

Gosfield

Gosfield is a very pleasant village of some 1000 inhabitants surrounded by beautiful parklands. It has welcomed a queen in her glory, sheltered a fugitive king, and has the largest fresh water lake in Essex.

The people have raised a large sum of money for the restoration of their beautiful church. The first church was built in 1190 by Aubrey de Vere, when the surrounding lands were owned by the Earls of Oxford, and this is why you will find the de Vere star on the north east buttress of the church wall, facing the lychgate. The present church was built by Sir Thomas Rolf in 1435.

Gosfield Hall began, in Tudor times, with a building by Sir John Wentworth in 1545, and was added to in the 17th and 18th centuries. There is some lovely English linenfold panelling in the Queen's Gallery and a priest's hole over the salon, which was often useful for eavesdropping! The hall also boasts an 18th century well and pumping system operated by a horse or donkey harnessed to a beam. There is only one other to be found in Britain, and that is believed to be on another old estate in the village known as 'Cut Edge', or Cut Hedge as it is now.

The lake, which was a small pond in Tudor times, was enlarged in the 18th century to a mile in length. It is now a tourist attraction, and used for water skiing training and national events.

There have been many distinguished visitors to the hall. Queen Elizabeth I really did stay there in 1561 and 1569. Louis XVIII of France spent two years of his exile at Gosfield Hall at the invitation of the Marquis of Buckingham, who then owned the hall. He often walked in the village and delighted the children by throwing pennies to them as he passed. Besides this, many of the villagers liked to go to the hall kitchens on Sundays, and sometimes in accordance with the French custom of the time, were even allowed in to see the King dine.

The King and his court were not the only French people living in Gosfield at that time. There was a small community of nuns, the Poor Clares, who had fled from France during the Revolution and who occupied a house called the Nunnery or Highgates in Church Road. They did much good in the village and gave the school children one halfpenny every Christmas. Ten of them are buried in the churchyard.

The Buckinghams, who owned the hall before moving to Stowe, brought many benefits to the village. They set up a school for all the poor children of the parish, gave a weekly dole to about 20 poor persons and a dinner every Sunday to the schoolchildren and other poor people.

Their greatest contribution was the setting up of a local industry plaiting straw for hats. Soon the industry flourished and skilled young girls were able to make a guinea a week, a fantastic sum in those days. It later moved and formed the basis of the straw hat industry at Luton.

After a rather chequered career the hall was sold in 1854 to Mr Samuel Courtauld, head of the textile firm. He brought a great many benefits to Gosfield and the district. His works at Bocking and Halstead brought an increase in employment and general prosperity. He built Park Cottages, the present primary school, the Coffee Room and many other cottages. In 1870 members of his family built the present building at Cut Hedge, together with the two lodges and other houses at White Ash Green for the servants, including a laundry.

One very recent benefactor of the village was Maurice Rowson. A bequest made by him made it possible to convert the old Sunday schoolroom to the present well appointed Maurice Rowson Hall which can be used for a multitude of functions. The rest of the money has been put into the Rowson Perpetual Memorial Fund for the benefit of the whole village. So Gosfield not only has an eventful past, but a flourishing present and future too.

Great Bardfield 🖄

Great Bardfield is a very attractive village having a wide, gently sloping High Street. Looking down from there one has a lovely view of the village greens, and the red brick Victorian school. There are over 800 names on the electoral register.

Bardfield has three places of worship which are all well attended. The parish church of St Mary has the world famous 14th century stone rood screen. Opposite is the modern Roman Catholic church of the Holy Spirit, built entirely by local workmen under the guidance of Charles Osbourne, dedicated in 1955 by the Bishop Beck of Brentwood. In the centre of the village is the Friends meeting house erected in 1804.

The house of special historical importance is Place House. It was built during the Tudor period and was once owned by William Bendlowes, who was Serjeant-at-Law to Queen Elizabeth I. Rumour has it that Elizabeth took refuge there when escaping the persecution of her sister Mary Tudor. Bendlowes left much of his wealth to the village and still in this present day, many young and old benefit from his charity trust. When repairs were being carried out, a Latin prayer was found tucked in a beam. This was written in the year 1665, and was asking protection from the plague.

Great Bardfield was granted a charter long ago so that a horse fair could be held during June. This was an annual two-day event which attracted horses from as far away as Wales, the Midlands and even Belgium and Holland. Horses were on the roads for weeks in order to reach Bardfield by 22nd June.

In 1955 Bardfield became known as 'The Artist's Village', as by that time many famous artists had settled here. Among them were John Aldridge, Edward Bawden, Michael Rothenstein, David Low and others. These artists opened their houses for a two-day festival and this attracted thousands of visitors. For many years now the Management Committee have kept up this tradition and organised a 'Spring Bank Holiday Festival'. This attracts artists and buyers from all the villages and towns around.

Great Bromley ⚜

Centuries ago a stream, now the Frating Brook, carved out a shallow valley and on its gentle northern slope rose in the 14th century one of the finest churches in Essex. It is the centre of the scattered village of Great Bromley and round it gather the one-time hall, now a Cheshire Home, the school, the post office-shop, the Spread Eagle, which closed as an inn in 1987, and a cluster of dwellings, some old, most new.

The road through the village comes from Dedham through Burnt Heath, a 'waste' when the church was young, but where there was the village forge. The smith was still working there 60 years ago.

Just across the brook Mary Lane branches off eastwards to Cowey Green, one of the village's three 'Green' outposts. A footpath from a bend in the lane, across the fields still exists and nearby, until they were condemned and pulled down some 60 years ago, were cottages called Guildhall and the Workhouse, which were of possibly Tudor origin.

Simon and Gregory Stone went from Great Bromley to a new life in New England in 1635. The brothers settled first at Watertown, a few miles up the Charles river from Boston, but after a year or so Gregory moved on to Cambridge, Massachusetts. Both became worthy citizens, as their memorials in their local churchyards proclaim. Some 270 years later their descendants gave them another memorial, the window in the church where they were baptised, St George's, Great Bromley.

In two lights stand St Simon the Apostle and St Gregory the Great. The increase decorates the top lights with the seals of Massachusetts and Essex, one to each side and in another stands an Indian. A Latin motto, translated, runs 'The generations pass into the coming generations', truly so of the Stones. Simon's and Gregory's descendants, though few still bear the name, now number more than 1000. Many of them visit their ancestral home and they maintain association with (to paraphrase) their forefathers' rude hamlet. Never a church appeal goes out but there is a generous response from Massachusetts and many other states.

Great Canfield

Great Canfield, mentioned in the Domesday Book in 1086, now has about 8 miles of road linking the four Ends which comprise Bacon End, Church End, Helman's Cross and Hope End. The old roads of Oak Lane (now called Cuckoo's Lane) and Boxley Lane were old drove roads.

The church, a Grade 1 listed building dates from the first part of the 12th century with the beautiful east wall mural of Mary and Child believed to have been completed in 1250. The mural was hidden during the Reformation by the memorial of the Wiseman family, but was re-discovered in 1879 when the memorial was removed for repairs and re-hung on the south wall. The Elizabethan chalice and paten used now only for special services are dated 1577.

The village stocks, last recorded in use in 1860 for a case of drunkenness have disappeared, but the whipping post remains at Helman's Cross. Elizabeth Abbot, who lived in Helman's was burnt as a witch in 1683.

During this century the hermit of Great Canfield lived out his solitary existence within a small wood, with few people seeing him and even fewer having any personal contact with him.

Although Great Canfield now has no school, shop or pub, the latter closing in the early part of this century, along with the school, the spirit and life of the village is alive and very active. Whether city commuter or farmer, the cricket club, WI, over 60s club or Canfield Society, all make great contributions to the activities, friendliness and unity of the village. The threat to English country life and prime farming land posed by the development of Stansted airport, still worries many villagers who are steadfast in their determination to try to protect and preserve the environment for the next 20 centuries.

Great Clacton 🐚

In the beginning Great Clacton was named Clacc-inga-ton, meaning 'the town of Clacc's people'. Over the centuries this name evolved to Clackintina, and later to Clackton Magna, which translates to Great Clacton.

Because the shoreline at that time was some distance further out to sea than it is today, Great Clacton was some three or four miles inland and was a farming community clustered round the old church of St John, which was built in the year 1108.

The area round the church was known as Church Square and all life was centred here. Remains have been found in the ground around the church which points to the probability that there was at one time a nunnery here and the certainty that a 'Cage' was in front of the church, into which wrong-doers were placed before sentence was passed on them. There were also a series of tunnels under the church which led to the Ship Inn, the Queens Head, and other places. One theory was that they were used by smugglers, who were very busy in this district.

The house now called St John's House was once the residence of the Bishop of London. The manor house was situated on the corner of what was St Osyth Main Road and the one time Butt Road, now London Road.

In the road now known as Valley Road, (formerly Little Holland Road) a fair was held on 29th June every year, outside the Ship Inn for 700 years. It was abolished in 1872.

Off to the right of this road was Bull Hill, where there was still a farmhouse during the 1940s. All the land around this farm has been taken over for the construction of the recreation ground, the council estate known as Windmill Park, and the land which is now occupied by Fiveways and other multiple businesses.

On the opposite side of 'Great Holland' or Valley Road, was the blacksmith's forge. The last smith there was named Wrigley. He still worked the ancient forge till the 1940s. Next in importance to the blacksmith came the saddler and harness maker. The last saddler was Mr Stearn who lived at No 5, now St Johns Road. From these cottages were all farm cottages in both directions, there being recorded that there were 45 tenant farmers and 50 smallholders around the district of Great Clacton. In the year 1801 the population of Great Clacton and Clacton numbered 904. In 1965 it numbered 32,550.

Bockings Elm is an area adjoining Great Clacton. The name was derived from the elm which stood, and has been replaced, on the triangle of St Johns Road and Little Clacton Road. The legend is that the highway robber named Bocking was hanged there.

Great Dunmow ✑

Great Dunmow lies in the heart of rural Essex. There has been a settlement here since the Iron Age when Dunmow developed as a Celtic watering place midway along the route, later known as Stane Street, connecting Colchester and St Albans, the two largest towns of that period. The Romans realised the importance of Dunmow and built a settlement at Church End and a garrison in the town. Many Roman remains have been found and can be viewed in Colchester Museum. The garrison and settlement were destroyed by Queen Boadicea in AD 70.

Many of the buildings on the High Street date from the Middle Ages. In 1380 a New Street was built to provide more homes for the shopkeepers and it still bears that name today!

The parish church of St Mary the Virgin is a church of great beauty dating back to 1280, although it lies on the foundations of a Saxon church. The largest building is the workhouse situated on Chelmsford Road, designed in 1840 to house 410 inmates. The architect, Sir George Gilbert Scott, was the brother of the local vicar. Amongst his other works are the Albert Memorial and St Pancras station.

There are many fine examples of domestic architecture in the town, clusters of old chimneys and plaster decorated with traditional designs. The Saracen's Cottage built in the late 17th century was used by the post boys attached to the Saracen's Head. The arms of the FitzWalter and Maynard families are seen in the pargetting. The present Electricity Showrooms, formerly Dove House, was the home of a Tudor wool merchant. The large central chimney with its open fireplace can be seen from the street.

In Market Square all of the buildings date from the Tudor period. At the end of the Causeway is Clock House built in the late 16th century. It is part brick, part timber framed and plastered, an important example of domestic architecture in Dunmow. Sir George Beaumont 1726–62 of Clock House, was instrumental in persuading the Government to present the Angerstein art collection to the nation, a move which led to the formation of the National Gallery in London.

Lionel Luckin, coachbuilder to the London elite, was born in Dunmow in 1742. He designed the first unsinkable lifeboat and tested it on the Doctors Pond in North Street in 1790.

The Catholic church of Our Lady and St Anne Line remembers the Dunmow widow Anne Line, who was hanged at Tyburn in 1601 for harbouring Jesuit priests.

A custom originating in Little Dunmow in 1140, The Dunmow Flitch, has, since 1949 taken place regularly every four years in Great Dunmow. Married couples swear, in a mock court presided over by a judge and jury of six maidens and six bachelors of the parish, that they have not quarrelled for a year and a day. A flitch of bacon is awarded to the winning couple who are paraded ceremoniously through the town in a special Flitch Chair.

Great Holland

The parish of Great Holland is a small village surrounded by sea, brook and railway, south-west of Frinton-on-Sea and is set in a wide expanse of flat, mostly arable farming country.

Public footpaths crisscross to and from neighbouring villages. These relics of old walkways are a source of pleasure for today's walkers and ramblers. Some 40 acres of this beautiful countryside is Essex Naturalist's Trust property, set aside as a nature reserve.

As a small community bordering the sea, Great Holland was a notorious place for smugglers in the 18th century. When a boat came ashore, the labourers assisted in 'working the goods' and frequently became addicted to alcohol with such constant supplies of gin. Several older properties including The Ship and the Lion's

Den are reputed to have cellars and passageways leading seawards for the concealment of the contraband.

Great Holland manor house was on the site of today's Manor Farm. It is known to have had a court held there in 1545 and to have been given for the use of Anne Boleyn's father, but the Ecclesiastical Court House in Little Clacton Road dated back to the 12th century.

The village has two churches. The Wesleyan Methodist church was built in 1928 at a cost of £3000. All Saints church dates back to the 13th century but, with the exception of the west tower, was rebuilt in 1866. The tower of red brick with black brick diapering is one of the best preserved in East Anglia.

Legend tells of Miss Barron, formerly a wealthy resident of nearby Walton-on-the-Naze, who in her advancing years became most eccentric and devoted to goats. Walton parish had approached the Barron Bell Trust for a peal of bells but, unfortunately for them, two of Miss Barron's goats strayed from her garden and wandered into the churchyard where they were seen by a passing churchwarden. He dispatched the goats with his boot but Miss Barron had witnessed the incident and in her indignation gave the peal of bells to Great Holland instead.

The Old Rectory built in 1830, now a private residence, boasts beautiful gardens. A very rare Turkey Oak tree survived when many majestic, mature trees were felled by the storm of October 1987. The annual Church Fete held in the grounds is an extremely popular event with visitors coming from far afield on the first Saturday of August.

The village green, now with its swings, slide and see-saw is well patronised by the younger generation, but 150 years ago it was used by the labourers as a donkey park. As many as 26 donkeys were left to graze on the green and 'the music from them was heard all over the parish'. Here it was traditional for bonfires, annual fairs and Methodist meetings to be held. The latter, preached from a borrowed farm wagon were well attended.

In 1975 East Essex Iron Works known as 'the Foundry' by the villagers and founded by the Ratcliffe family, finally came to a halt after almost a century of the very specialised production of cast, chilled ploughshares, distributed worldwide.

Across the road is the village hall built by the local residents in 1909. The village stores and post office is the only shop remaining of a butchery, dairy, general stores, bicycle repairer, second-hand shop, post office and milliners, all trading in the early 1900s.

The present population of 800 is steadily increasing. No longer is it a farming community. With the advent of modern machinery the labour force has dwindled to an expert few.

Great Horkesley ✤

The lovely little 12th century parish church of All Saints, stands on the northern boundary of the village on a hill overlooking the Stour valley and Suffolk beyond.

Yet the village pre-dates the church by many centuries for Great Horkesley is one of the oldest inhabited places in the country, with Iron Age earthworks still to be seen in Pitchbury Wood and very early tiles and pottery, made from the local clay, discovered within the parish. Roman coins have turned up in field and garden and there is a legend that Queen Boadicea fought a battle near Pitchbury Wood. The long straight road that slashes through Horkesley from north to south is a Roman road and was itself superimposed upon an ancient time-worn track.

The name Horkesley means 'a shelter for lambs' and the village has always been an agricultural area and remains so today. In earlier times the houses were largely at the northern end, but building has gradually moved southward towards Colchester. Recent housing developments have brought an increase in population and local life flourishes, with an active church and thriving school, and a wide variety of clubs and organisations.

Great Horkesley has a quite undramatic history but sometimes a controversial character has appeared in its midst, ruffling placid waters. During the 18th century just such a person became rector of Great Horkesley. He was the Reverend John Brown who was presented to the living in 1756 by his patron, Lord Hardwicke. John Brown was highly gifted: a scholar, a dramatist, a poet as well as a churchman.

In 1756, the village was very small, with a population of 450. It was a place of farms and farm-workers, small tradesmen and craftsmen. With the exception of two Quaker families living at Spratts Marsh the village people were Church of England. In general life was peaceful and in step with the rhythm of the seasons.

Unfortunately such a simple rural environment did not suit John Brown's volatile temperament and soon after his arrival in Great Horkesley his parishioners were complaining that he spent too much of his time in London.

And so he did. Whilst he was rector of Great Horkesley Brown wrote two major plays, *Barbarossa* and *Aethelstane*, both of them tragedies, which were produced at Drury Lane Theatre with the famous actor David Garrick himself appearing in them.

John Brown was rector for five years and left in 1761 for the living of St Nicholas in Newcastle. He continued to write on his favourite subjects, music, politics and education amongst them, and his last undertaking was an ambitious plan for popular education in Russia.

He is almost forgotten now but taken all in all he must be one of the most remarkable people ever to have lived in Great Horkesley.

Great Oakley 🦡

A settlement at Great Oakley has been in existence since 3000 BC. A primitive pot dating from that period was found south of the village during the 1950s and it is now to be seen in Colchester castle. The village became known as Acley, which means 'oak pasture', when the Saxons invaded and settled in the area. Then the Normans came and the village was surveyed, and it was listed in the Domesday Book of 1086, under the name of Acclei.

There are many oak trees still standing in and around the village, even after the loss of many during the great storm of 1987. Oak trees from Great Oakley were taken to Harwich to be used in ship building, so Great Oakley's oak trees no doubt travelled the world when ships were still made of wood and really were 'hearts of oak'.

The village still boasts an industry which sends a commodity over the world and that is an explosives factory. It is housed on an island in the Hamford Waters, north-east of the village. Bramble Island, linked to the mainland by a causeway, was acquired by the Explosives Company in 1905. It was a small affair at first. Cases of explosives were ordered three or four at a time and these were loaded on to a cart and drawn by horse to Thorpe le Soken station, six miles away and sent off by train. Later a dock was constructed and barges were used. The First World War caused the factory to step up production considerably, so it made a great contribution to the war effort. Then again in the Second World War its goods were in great demand.

There have been a number of accidental explosions at the factory, one in 1942 when three employees died and three of the workers were awarded the Edward Medal later converted to the George Cross. In the east coast floods of 1953, three employees received awards for their bravery in disposing of explosives left in a very dangerous condition by the rising tides. For their courage they received the British Empire Medal.

In the early 1900s Great Oakley was a large and thriving community, with many shops, good communication between Harwich Clacton and Colchester.

In the early 1920s there were many activities in the village, such as a football and a cricket team. There was even a ladies football team! It was reported at one time, in the local paper however, that the goalkeeper had to play for her team in a long skirt because her husband would not allow her to wear shorts. Fancy going for the ball in a skirt!

Great Totham 🦋

Great Totham is recorded in Domesday Book, and Court Rolls from the 13th and 15th centuries exist, mentioning Gibecrakes Farm and Fabians Farm which still remain today although the old Gibecrakes farmhouse has been replaced by a new dwelling. Totham Hall was a moated manor house with a long history, but as it was completely modernised in 1825 it does not have the appearance of an ancient hall.

Great Totham is a very large parish, which includes the Island of Osea in the Blackwater estuary. The village is long, consisting of two parts separated by about a mile and a half.

The south part of the village contains the lovely St Peter's church, dating back to Norman times. There is also the Barn Chapel, with its thatched roof, which became a chapel in 1822 when Mr Isaac Foster donated his barn for a place of worship for non-conformists after hearing John Raven, a ploughman, preaching to his fellow workers.

The village school celebrated its centenary in 1977, but by that time the Victorian building, though still in existence and used for storage, had been replaced by a large modern school on a different site. There is also a Grade II listed building known as the Honywood School founded in the mid 19th century as a church school by the Honywood family of Marks Hall, Coggeshall who had inherited the manor of Great Totham. This is still in use as the church hall.

The main village hall, built in the 1930s is always busy. There are also three thriving pubs in this part of the village, The Crown, The Bull and the Prince of Wales. The Post Office Stores is in the centre of the village.

In Great Totham North there is a United Reformed church dating from 1871, recently refurbished and used not only for services but for many other activities such as the pre-school playgroup. Just around the corner adjoining the small village green, are the village shop and the late 17th century Compasses pub.

According to the old maps, before the time of the enclosures, the outskirts of Great Totham North were part of Tiptree Heath, then well known as a haunt of smugglers, this being celebrated in the name of a house in Mountains Road, Spirits Hall. The 'mountain' in question is Beacon Hill, at 83 metres one of the highest points in the county and probably the original place of settlement, giving the name Totham, possibly derived from the Saxon, meaning 'look out' or 'hill top dwelling'.

Over the years the village has produced many characters and a few celebrities. There was until after the Second World War a very successful tug-of-war team consisting entirely of brothers, the Barber family. Today it can boast of John Doubleday, the sculptor, whose 'Beatles' sculpture in Liverpool is well known.

Perhaps the most memorable of all, however, was Sir Claude Champion de Crespigny. Born in London in 1847, Sir Claude lived for many years at Champion Lodge in Great Totham. In 1883, accompanied by Joseph Simmons, an aeronaut, the adventurous baronet crossed the Channel in a hot air balloon which he had christened *The Colonel*.

Great Wakering ✍

Great Wakering is one of several village communities living in the green and pleasant marsh-lands of south-east Essex. The village has been constantly inhabited since prehistoric times, and was an important small town or large fort during the Roman occupation. The name of Wakering is thought to have originated during the Saxon period from the name of its owner, Walchel or Walcher, and the word 'ing' which means meadow or pasture.

The Romans produced much of their salt here, by creating evaporation tanks, large vessels beneath which, fires would reduce readily available sea-water. As this method of extraction declined, the abandoned sites and apparatus gradually disintegrated, leaving the area covered with burnt red-clay, thus giving rise to sites now known as Red-hills. The available clay was also used in brick-making, an industry that has been carried on in the village over many centuries.

The area being marsh-land, was very damp and supported many associated diseases which were particularly detrimental to women. This, plus the appalling death rate of women through childbirth etc, created a deficit of females, and replacements were persuaded to come from the more northerly counties to make up the short-fall. While being damp, the average rainfall is the lowest in the country, and Great Wakering's greatest current claim to fame, is to be entered in the *Guinness Book of Records*, as the 'Driest Place in the United Kingdom'.

The sea has always played an important role in the life of the village. Apart from its harvest of fish, oysters and wildfowl, it enabled the village to transport its surplus products to various markets and to import other essentials, such as spirits, tobacco, silks etc, that is provided the Customs men did not get there first, for the winding shallow creeks were a haven for smugglers.

The area is rich in stories of witchcraft, ghosts and superstition, much of which is centred on the parish church of St Nicholas. The nave and chancel are said to have been built about 1100 while the tower, porches etc were added over the following centuries. It is thought that the church is at least the second such structure to stand on the site, replacing a Saxon church which served as the burial place of two murdered princes, Ethelbert and Ethelred.

Amongst the ghosts of the area is Clement the baker who hanged himself from a tree situated at a road junction, known as 'Baker's Grave', and in keeping with the practice of the time would no doubt have been buried in the highway with a stake through his body.

Apart from the church and Little Wakering Hall, the area now has few old buildings, as most of them were made of wood which readily rots in the damp atmosphere.

The modern community endeavours to maintain a village atmosphere, while supporting a substantial number of social, educational and recreational groups, most of which participate in the annual village fair, this being a re-establishment of the ancient fair granted by charter to the village in the 13th century. The village is justly proud of its accommodation for the elderly, and its Helping Hands Service for which it was awarded first prize in the Essex County Competition of 1986.

Great Waltham 🪶

Once known as Waltham Magna, the village lies five miles north of Chelmsford, and is about halfway between London and Cambridge. The village, which retains much of its old architecture (the Historic Monuments Commission having noted more than 80 old houses within the bounds of the parish) has extended its housing considerably twice since the Second World War, and now numbers among its residents many commuters to London, changing the pre-war, almost solely farming village into a very mixed community.

The church of St Mary and St Lawrence with its peal of eight bells, the oldest cast in 1336 and the newest in 1769, contains traces of Norman work incorporating Roman bricks. The Norman font bowl was discovered under the floor in the restoration of 1961 and is now in the porch, and the stair doorway and windows in the tower are Norman. The roof of the nave, with its hammer beam trusses carved with angels, is about 450 years old. On the right of the nave at the back are pews dating from about 1420 and, as such, are among the oldest in the country. A panel listing the names of vicars from 1361 can be seen on the south wall and includes the eminent historian Nicholas Tindal who had Philip

Morant, the historian of Essex, as his curate from 1722 to 1732. It also includes Canon Hulton (1876–1906) whose benefactions to church and parish include the village hall, the almshouses, the schoolmaster's house (now a private house opposite the school) and much else.

The church contains a magnificent memorial dated 1611 to Sir Richard Everard and his wife Anne (a cousin of Oliver Cromwell) in alabaster and marble.

Langleys lies in its own park to the north-west of the village. The estate we see today began when the manor was owned in 1200 by a family named Mariskall or Marshall. From the Mariskall's the house came under the ownership in the middle of the 14th century of the Langley's, the name being retained until the present day. The Everard family were there for over 200 years and it then came into the possession of the Tufnell's, who were responsible for enlarging the house and converting it into a gracious Queen Anne house.

The parish of Great Waltham is said to be one of the largest in England and includes the hamlets of Broads Green, Howe Street, Ford End and North End and bounds the medieval village of Pleshey on one side. The village itself contains two large Tudor houses, Wisemans which is reputed to have a priest's hole, and the one known to the village as The Guildhall which has magnificent Tudor chimneys and can be seen just before the church when entering the village from Chelmsford. The vicarage, opposite the west front of the church is a pleasant Queen Anne house of red brick.

There are a number of old cottages, mostly surrounding the church, one of which houses the bakehouse, still producing excellent bread, cakes and pastries as it has for more than 150 years by descendants of the first baker. At the beginning of the century there was a thriving lace industry but now there is little other industry apart from the workings of a gravel pit near Broads Green. There are four public houses in the village listed in 1769 and all still selling ale and spirits.

There was a trial of at least one witch in the 16th century. Elizabeth Lowys or Lewys, was tried as a witch in 1563, was found guilty but pleaded pregnancy. During her examination she admitted to having a herb garden – a fairly innocuous occupation in the 20th century!

Great Warley 🌿

Great Warley's most famous inhabitant was Miss Ellen Willmott (1858–1934), a distinguished horticulturist whose home Warley Place stood with pride in beautiful grounds in the village. Her name has been given to many species of flowers, particularly roses. She became the first women fellow of the Linnean Society of London, also first woman holder of the Victoria Medal of Honour created by the Royal Horticultural Society to honour the Diamond Jubilee.

Warley Place at one time stood on the main road to Brentwood but later a new road was made to enable the house to overlook a large field which is a colourful sight every spring with masses of mauve and yellow crocus, snowdrops followed by daffodils.

During the hurricane in 1987 many rare and priceless trees were damaged or destroyed but every effort is being made to restore the grounds to a pleasant area once more by the Essex Naturalists' Trust.

Records of the village date back to 1538 when Great Warley was known as the manor of Warle, Abbess Warley or Warley Magna under the ruling of the Abbess of Barking.

The old church became unusable and a temporary wooden building was erected. The present parish church of St Mary the Virgin, built in 1902 in memory of Arnold Heseltine, was erected by Mr Evelyn Heseltine, his brother. This is classed as Art Noveau with settings of mother-of-pearl and aluminium.

Coombe Lodge, an impressive country house originally owned by the Ind family, became the property of Mr E Heseltine and was used as a hospital for wounded soldiers during the First World War. During the Second World War it was again occupied by the RAF. Great Warley was also a 'bomb alley' for enemy planes discarding their loads on return journeys and many parts of the village suffered casualties and damage to buildings, including the church hit more than once.

The village is one of the few with an active blacksmith's forge and in bygone days boasted a brick works at Stoneyhills, with a carpenter and wheelwright around the village green, which was converted into a delightful residence now known as Chestnut Tree Cottage.

Village life has changed dramatically since the opening of the new M25 a few miles away. The estate workers' farms and cottages have been modernised and value of property in the area greatly increased, now privately owned.

The main residence of the village The Goldings, home of the late Mr Evelyn Heseltine, stands in 12 acres of beautiful grounds and has an organ built about 1860, one of only three built by French craftsmen. This was converted to The New World Inn in 1969, whilst Coombe Lodge has become a residential home for the elderly.

Greenstead Green 🌿

Greenstead Green lies just two miles to the south of Halstead. One villager remembers life here just after the First World War. 'In the 1920s Greenstead Green was a self contained village. We had a local builder and blacksmith. The blacksmith was very important when our iron hoops required mending. There was no electricity and no piped water. The children earned their pocket money by carrying buckets of water from the pump for people.

There was a school that children attended until they were 14. The village was ruled by the two schoolmistresses with help from the local vicar. We had our seasons for ball games, spinning tops and bowling hoops. There were about three cars in the village so most of our games took place in the road.

The church played a great part in our lives. Sunday meant church in the morning and Sunday school in the afternoon. We were not allowed to play games or to sing songs on Sunday. Good Friday was church in the morning and primrose gathering in the afternoon with our Sunday school teacher. The primroses that we gathered helped to decorate the church for Easter. Rogation Sunday and the congregation and the robed choir went into the fields to bless the growing crops.

Nearly all the village joined in for the Harvest Festival. The largest potatoes, marrows, carrots and onions were carefully put on one side to decorate the church. The church was always full for the harvest services, with everyone joining in the familar harvest hymns.

The annual flower show that took place in the grounds of the local Hall was an eagerly contested affair. There would be two or three huge tents and often very critical remarks were passed. Races in the afternoon for the children, dancing on the lawn in the evening and to finish the festivities off, a magnificent display of huge fireworks including 'The Prince of Wales feathers'.

Greensted-juxta-Ongar

Greensted parish is well known for its ancient Saxon church, the oldest wooden church in the world. Every year thousands of people from overseas and Great Britain visit this lovely little church. At least one service is held there every Sunday, and worship has continued for 1300 years!

The Church of St Andrew, Greensted

The church was probably built on the site of a pagan 'temple' by Saxon settlers before they were converted to Christianity by St Cedd. Cedd began his work in about AD 645 and the first church at Greensted was probably built soon after that date. The church is dedicated to St Andrew also suggesting a Celtic foundation. The nave was probably added about AD 845. Dark patches on some of the present upright wall timbers may be scorch marks from lamps or torches. The flat inner sides of the logs were smoothed by adzes.

The parish is small and rural and the church has a peaceful setting. At one time Greensted had two mills, one a windmill, and the other a watermill: no trace of them remain today. There was once also a large open green, and although the postal address remains Greensted Green, the green has been enclosed and taken into adjoining land.

Between Greensted church and the Drill House Inn at a T-junction is Drapers Corner. It is claimed that nearly 200 years ago a man named Draper was hanged there for stealing sheep – his ghost still haunts this corner!

Close to the church is Greensted Hall, the site of a Saxon manor. The present house dates from the 15th century and was altered by Alexander Cleeve whose initials are seen on the front facade. It later belonged to the Budworth family, descendants of the Cleeves and whose memorials are in the church.

The village has connections with the Tolpuddle Martyrs. Six Dorset farm labourers were given harsh sentences for agitating for higher wages and better working conditions by forming a trade union at Tolpuddle. After their conviction in 1834 they were condemned to transportation to Australia for seven years. In England there was a public outcry at their harsh treatment and sentences, and eventually their sentences were commuted in 1837.

They were unable to resettle in Dorset owing to the farmers' opposition, so they were granted farm tenancies in Greensted juxta Ongar and High Laver. One of their tenancies was for Newhouse Farm, Greensted Green. The land was in poor condition and difficult to farm – one of the fields is still known as 'Starve Goose Field'! While in Greensted James Brine married the daughter of a fellow prisoner, Elizabeth Stanfield. The 'martyrs' tenancies were not renewed owing to local opposition and they emigrated to Canada.

Hadleigh 🎐

Investigations indicate that a settlement here was inhabited during the early Iron Age. The name Hadleigh goes back to Saxon times.

Hadleigh has two prominent edifices. The first is the church which was built about 1140 by the Normans and probably takes the place of an earlier timber structure. It stands on top of a hill and is older than Hadleigh castle, the other famous building. The interior of the church has some interesting features, the most important being a wall painting of Thomas a Becket thought to have been painted in 1170 or 1171.

It was Henry III who granted a Royal Licence to Hubert de Burgh to build the castle in 1231. In 1539 Henry VIII gave the castle to Anne of Cleves and later to his last Queen Catherine Parr. By the 17th century it had become ruinous. It has been immortalised by John Constable, the famous painter.

A tunnel was supposed to link the castle with the Castle Inn, a mile distant, and contraband is said to have poured into the village via this subterranean route. There is certainly an ancient cellar at the inn, but a tunnel that length would have been a major engineering feat. Its existence was probably more imaginary than factual.

It is known, however, that the Castle Inn, then called the Boar's Head, was used as a hide-out for smugglers and their goods. And when demobilised soldiers and their wives settled in the wooded district after the Napoleonic wars, smuggling and crime made the area notorious.

Things changed with the arrival of the Peculiar People, who took their name from a Bible text: 'the Lord hath chosen thee to be a peculiar people' (Deut 14 v2). They converted the populace to agriculture and a more settled way of life.

This dedicated sect is now called the Union of Evangelical Churches. Just one of their three churches remains. It is a small building, but an even smaller place of worship is the little timber-built St Michael's church at the corner of St Michael's Road and Bramble Road. About 90 years old, it can hold 50 people at a pinch. Set in a green woodland setting, it would be a tourist attraction if it were not so far off the beaten track.

Hadleigh's most famous citizen in the 19th century was Wizard

Cunning Murrell who cured people's ailments by a combination of incantation and herbalism. In his working life he was a shoemaker, but colourful tales are still told of him being involved with smuggling, witchcraft, fortune-telling, magic and astronomy.

The Salvation Army has played a major part in the history of Hadleigh, and their band plays most Sunday mornings in its streets. Some 3,000 acres of wooded slopes around Hadleigh castle were bought in 1890 by General Booth and a farm colony started. Ex-Borstal boys, people on probation, and problem cases of all kinds, passed through the gates on which were emblazoned the words: 'Enter His Courts With Praise'. They were taught farming skills, and for most of them it was just the break with their past life that they needed.

Hadstock 🦢

The village is formed around the meeting point of three ancient travel ways, resulting in a basic three star plan centred on the village green and dominated by the parish church. In pre-medieval times when the water table was higher the Linton Road was a river, all that remains is a ditch on the south side. In the floods of September 1968 the river reverted, and for two or three days it gave a dramatic view of what it must have been like. The road is still liable to flooding.

The oldest building is the Anglo Saxon church. It is said to be sited at the meeting point of 16 ley lines. Dedicated to St Botolph, one time patron saint of travellers, it is said to be his monastery, which he founded in 654 and in which he was buried. The church's other claim to fame is having been built by the Danes. Its ruins were restored by King Canute to commemorate those slain in the Battle of Assendun in 1016. The north door is the oldest door in use in the country. It is dated about 1020. It was said that a Dane tried to steal the church plate, was caught and flayed alive and his skin nailed to the door as a warning. When the door was mended a piece of skin was found under a hinge. This proved to be of a fair-haired man going grey and can be seen in Saffron Walden Museum.

In early medieval times Hadstock was quite an important town with an annual horse fair on St Botolph's Day, 17th June, and a weekly market. These fairs were confirmed by Charter of Henry I and were first granted by Edward the Confessor. The Charter was annulled by Act of Parliament on the petition of the then rector in the late 19th century owing to having degenerated into a lower class drunken brawl. It was revived in 1950 as the annual church fete on the Saturday nearest St Botolph's Day. By the 13th century Hadstock's importance had begun to decline owing to the church tower's collapse and later to the Black Death. However Hills Road (the A604 out of Cambridge) was called the Hadstock Road and Newmarket Races has its Hadstock Handicap.

Up to 1950 the village population of about 300 was mostly agricultural but it has now only one farmer and one tractor driver, people finding work in Cambridge, Linton, Saffron Walden and London.

Hadstock is still a beautiful village and has won the Essex Best Kept Small Village competition in 1970 and 1986. It has many old properties several of the 15th century, one had a priest's hole and 34 are listed.

Hatfield Broad Oak

Approached along winding country roads and lanes, Hatfield Broad Oak is an ancient roadside village, a compact village with a definite beginning and an end.

Enter the village at half-light, when narrow roads and pavements blend into one with silhouettes of uneven pitched roofs and bulging walls of timbered buildings, and it is not difficult to glimpse back to medieval times. An exhausting clamber to the top of the historic church tower, now standing some 81 feet, reveals a remarkable view of roof-tops and an intricate, mis-shapen patchwork of outhouses and gardens, which finally interlock with one another as the pattern of a jigsaw. Certainly not the dream of modern planners, but a rare insight into early building skills and craftmanship. Missing now is the Benedictine monastery with cloistered courtyard, as are the old houses which once thrust their way into the high street to enclose the Town Square.

In January 1877 at the village pump the usual gatherings occurred – a lamp stood on top of the pump at little more than head height, and it was a good place to exchange news at all times.

On that day there was an irrepressible air of expectancy and much to-ing and fro-ing at The Plume of Feathers, opposite.

The ongoing cause of gossip related to the frequency, under circumstances of a most suspicious nature, of incendiarism in the district. The old village fire engine was in a state of disrepair and had ceased to be available for active service and it had been decided to provide a new fire engine for the use of the parish – with a fire engine ladder and fire escape! A suitable engine had been chosen and was to be sent from Long Acre in London this very day!

This grand occasion was reported in *The Herts and Essex Observer* at the end of the week, as follows:

'No event since the Prince of Wales's marriage in March 1863 has excited more public interest in this parish than the inauguration of the NEW FIRE ENGINE.

Outside the village the engine was met and decked with flags and at the bottom of Feathers Hill a halt was called while the newly appointed brigade fell in behind in twos, a blue rosette being served to each man. The further passage of the engine through the village partook of the nature of a triumphal procession. The top of the hill at the Feathers was crowded with people and there was scarcely a person in the place who did not glimpse the engine as it passed their doors. The church bells, too, rang out most merrily in honour of the occasion.'

Helions Bumpstead

Helions Bumpstead is situated in the north western corner of Essex, on the borders of Suffolk and Cambridgeshire. In 1066 the mighty armies of William, Duke of Normandy, invaded England, and gifts of land were given to his officers. Such an officer was Tihel, a captain of the rear-guard who was given the land called Bumsted.

The name Bumsted came from the Saxon word 'bune' meaning a hollow stem and 'sted' meaning place. Rushes have hollow stems and grew in abundance alongside the little stream which flows through the village. It is stated that Tihel came from a village called Hellean in the Morbihan department of Brittany, and it is believed that the Helion family, whom we first hear living at Helions manor a hundred years later were his descendants. Hence the name Helions Bumpstead.

Helions' church stands on a mound in the centre of the village, with a brick tower rising high enough to be seen as one approaches the village from almost any direction. Although a rather plain and simple church inside, it is a building that achieves a great beauty for sound. No list of the vicars of the church exists, but those known of date back from the beginning of the early 13th century.

It is known that weaving and spinning were carried out in the village and cheesemaking continued here until the 18th century.

High Easter 🐑

The ancient village of High Easter possibly derives its name from the old English 'eowestre' meaning 'sheepfold' and the 'high' probably from its situation on the hill. The highest point in the parish is 287 feet which is about 27 feet higher than the highest point at Good Easter. Situated between the county town of Chelmsford and Great Dunmow, its fascinating history lies in the evolution of its dwellings, facilities and services throughout the centuries.

The village was well served by schools, the British school where pupils paid 1d a week and the Church of England school, now a private residence. There were general stores which included an off-licence kept by Mr Lodge who also had a bicycle shop and acted as a carrier. The butcher's shop called the Cock and Rother-shop was sited on the left hand side as one enters the churchyard.

The workhouse, now two private houses, saw coffins carried along the back fields path to the church past the Cock and Bell. This inn had a bake house by the tap room door. Together with The Punchbowl opposite, they still bear witness to their 15th century origins.

Men of distinction had their lives entwined with High Easter. The years 1649–1662 saw Martin Holbeach as vicar. A famous headmaster at Felsted school, he had two brilliant mathematicians among his pupils – Isaac Barrow, who as the first Lucasian Professor of Mathematics in 1663 resigned in favour of Isaac Newton in 1669, and John Wallis, one of the founders of the

Royal Society who invented the method of imparting the art of speech to deaf mutes.

In the beautiful nave roof above the clerestory in the church, a carved gate can be seen and it is said to be a rebus on the name of Sir Geoffrey Gate, who died in 1526. The illustrious family of Gate lived at Great Garnetts, in an old house since pulled down and of which only the moated site remains. The last of the family to live there was Sir John Gate, appointed Gentleman of the Privy Chamber by Henry VIII in 1535. He was made Knight of the Bath, became Sheriff of Essex in 1549 and three years later became Chancellor of the Duchy of Lancaster. On the death of Edward VI in 1553 he supported the celebrated devise of succession in favour of Lady Jane Grey. For that he was arrested, tried and found guilty and was beheaded on Tower Hill on August 22, 1553.

A late example of witchcraft in the country is the case in 1880 of Charles Brewster and his son Peter versus Levi Sharpe, a labourer of High Easter on behalf of his wife, Susan. They accused her of bewitching the son's wife and said that to prove her guilt, which she stoutly denied, she must submit to being thrown into one of the village ponds. If she sank, they would be satisfied she was not a witch 'for witches could always swim'.

Father and son were told by the chairman of the court they had been guilty of 'a very foolish act' and each was bound over in his own recognizances of £5 to keep the peace for six months!

Hockley 🦡

The ancient village of Hockley stands on high ground, commanding a view of the river Crouch. It has two high points, on Plumberow Mount Roman remains have been found and the other is dominated by the parish church.

Hockley, which means mallow field, was purely agricultural and has survived the Saxons, the Danish invasions, the Normans and the Black Death as so many other Essex villages have done. The present church, of St Peter and St Paul was built in 1220 on a Saxon foundation. During one of the restorations an ancient Norman altar stone was unearthed and it is now used as a requiem altar. During the reign of Mary Tudor, the curate William Tyms was burned at Smithfield, martyred for his faith.

The ancient manor has been held by various people important in history, from the Abbess of Barking, to Thomas Cromwell, the Crown, Anne of Cleves and the Earls of Warwick.

The lot of the poor tenants and the labourers was hard. With the land enclosures life became even harder and many ended their days in the poorhouse which stood on Hockley Common. The common itself and the old smithy have gone, but the Bull Inn which was opposite still stands.

With the coming of the turnpike road in 1747 a tollgate was erected and the stagecoaches came through on their way to Rochford from Shenfield, and the village began to grow. The old fountain, although only a symbol now, still stands at the top of Fountain Lane, where the horses could drink before going into the village.

In 1838 a 'curing' spring was discovered and three years later a spa was established. An imposing Romanesque pump room was built. Unfortunately the spa failed, mainly as the fashion was now for sea bathing. The Spa Hotel was built, but there were not enough amenities to sustain the popularity of taking the waters and the enterprise failed. The spa building still remains, now a listed building and in the care of Guinness Brothers who make billiard tables.

Nearby stands a thatched cottage, built in 1635, now known as the China Cottage, which was decorated by a former owner, Mr Harry Prior with pieces of smashed china. Mr Prior, member of a well known local family, spent much of his time purchasing odd china to add to his decorative cottage.

The National school, which stood next to the church, was moved to the main village in 1904. The old schoolroom has been converted into a private house, but still keeps the school bell in the roof.

The railway, which arrived in 1889, cut the parish church off from the main village and signalled the growth of Hockley. Farms were sold and more houses were built. There are still some farms left although most residents now commute to London, Southend or Chelmsford.

The village is lucky that it still has woodlands. Hockley Woods, with their stories of witchcraft and where the charcoal burners plied their trade, still bears the scars of jettisoned bombs during the Battle of Britain. Unfortunately the trees were terribly damaged during the 1987 hurricane.

Holland-on-Sea 🌿

Holland-on-Sea, situated between Clacton and Frinton, is a small resort referred to by locals as The Village. Its name is a derivative of Little Holland by which it was known way back in the 13th century.

Round about the end of the 15th century Holland was referred to in records as a small parish dotted with bungalows and wooden shacks. At that period each lord of the manor claimed his royal prerogative and confiscated any wreck which happened to get stranded on the shore. The flat Essex coastline from Sandy Point to beyond Cheveaux Point was an ideal beach for smugglers of French brandy and other contraband to land their boats. Often this stretch of the coast took a battering from the elements.

The parish was divided into privately owned plots and estates, two being the Kings Cliff and Preston Park estates. Of later years one privately owned section of the cliffs was reinforced with concrete because of encroachment by the sea and erosion of the cliffs which were also riddled with rabbit holes. Eventually the council took control of the cliffs and beach.

Holland has developed to the extent that very little land is available for building purposes. Blocks of flats have changed the skyline of the rather flat area.

Little Holland Hall, a stately home of earlier centuries is within sight of the sea. A Grade 2 listed house, it was formerly lived in by lords of the manor. The grounds reach up to the main Frinton road. Adjacent to the road is an old Saxon cemetery where a few years ago the skeleton of a tall Viking with a hole in his forehead was excavated along with Roman remains. Beneath the orchard are some remains of the old village.

Horndon-on-the-Hill 🌿

There are many ghost stories told in this ancient and historical village. One 20th century ghost story recorded in the parish register concerns a lady called Mrs Oman, who used to rise out of a pond riding on a donkey. This apparition would cross the road and disappear into the coppice on the other side of the road, causing many cyclists to swerve and have accidents. Her haunting was about 300 yards north of the old road junction at Rookery Corner. Another ghost, a man, used to ride a horse at speed from Orsett Road down along Blackbush Lane; this apparition was also blamed for accidents at this junction.

Thomas Higbed of Horndon House, in March 1555, met his death by burning at a stake in the centre of the village. Thomas Higbed was a yeoman with a very puritanical outlook. When Queen Mary succeeded to the throne, she was determined to re-establish Catholicism, aided and advised by Bishops Pole and Bonner. Bishop Bonner held an estate at Orsett and George Tyrell betrayed Thomas Higbed to him.

Situated about 150 yards to the east of the 12th century church of St Peter and St Paul, is the 15th century inn called The Bell. It is here since about 1900, that on Good Friday each year, a hot cross bun, freshly baked, is hung from one of the original oak beams. This task is usually performed by one of the oldest residents in the village, as a mark of esteem. The row of buns now extends for the length of the beam and many of them are blackened with age. In 1941, during the Second World War, no buns were baked due to a shortage of ingredients but a replacement bun was hung, made of concrete.

The origins of the annual Feast and Fayre taking place on the last weekend in June, date back to the granting of a Royal Charter to Robert Gifford and his heirs in perpetuity by King Edward I. Although changing form throughout the centuries the Fayre continued until the early years of the century. Revived by the Horndon Society in 1974 and taking a different historical period as a theme each year, it has become a feature of the village, giving an opportunity to promote the revival of interest in crafts, support for local and charitable organisations, and quite simply to provide a festive occasion for all to enjoy.

Ingatestone

It was reported as hurricane force winds that night in October 1987, which had torn and smashed the trees to the ground. The local residents of Ingatestone viewed the scene with unbelieving shock and a feeling of helplessness. Those beautiful, majestic sentinels had stood tall with history passing beneath their out-stretched branches for possibly hundreds of years.

It is possible those same trees stood there in 1742 when the physicians rushed to attend the 8th Baron Petre, who was dying of smallpox. Though only 29 years of age, he was a brilliant botanist and garden expert. His interest starting as a young boy, he later travelled to all parts of the world in his search for specimens, and

The clock tower, Ingatestone Hall

we have him to thank for many of the trees and shrubs to be found in our gardens today, to name but one, the michaelmas daisy.

Smallpox was once rife in Essex – hundreds of families suffered and were wiped out. In the year 1766 Ingatestone villagers may have had their doubts about 'cures' for the scourge. However, there was one man who moved into their midst who had discovered otherwise. He was Daniel Sutton, England's greatest inoculator and his treatment had brought about the decline of the dreaded disease.

John Troughton must have felt gratitude for the strength of the oak's timber which had built his ship *The Lioness* as he crashed through the thrashing waves of the Mediterranean Sea, in engagements against the Spanish and Portuguese in the 1600s. Then a Commander he had started his career as a page to the Petre family at the Hall. A plaque placed in the parish church by the family, to his memory, can be seen today.

A warning to each generation has been not to stand under a tree in a storm for fear of lightning striking, but did those turkey drovers hesitate to do so, as they journeyed in all weathers from Norfolk to Romford market. Some of them might have been lucky and been given shelter for the night in stables, perhaps at the Bell Inn or one of the others of which there were many.

Dawn would find them making an early start on the highway, keeping a careful watch on the livestock and listening for the resounding trumpeting of a horn, which would announce the rapid oncoming of the Royal Mail coach, on its way to London from Ipswich at 12 miles an hour!

Ingrave

The village of Ingrave is two miles south of Brentwood. It lies by the lovely woodlands of Thorndon Hall, the former family seat of Lord Petre, who remains closely interested in the manor. The A128 passes through Herongate and East Horndon, now all in the parish of Ingrave, to the A127, the Southend Road.

The present church of St Nicholas, built of red brick, is one of the most remarkable 18th century churches in the county. It has a massive west tower, holding six bells. It was built by the Roman Catholic Lord Petre of the time for the Protestant workmen on his estate, which was compulsory as the previous two churches, both dedicated to St Nicholas, had fallen into ruins.

William Byrd, the famous Elizabethan composer and organist, one of the fathers of English music, is recorded as having stayed with Lord Petre at old Thorndon Hall three times. He later settled at Stondon Massey, where he died in 1623. Vaughan Williams visited Ingrave in 1903 when collecting old folk songs for posterity. His lovely song *Bushes and Briars* was recorded here.

The second of the old churches stood in Rectory Lane, now Middle Road, opposite which still stands the old rectory (circa 1600). It was renamed 'Heatleys' after the Rev Henry Heatley, the last incumbent to live there.

Rising above the Southend Road is the medieval church of All Saints, East Horndon. It is steeped in the history of the Tyrell family and contains an incised slab of the tomb of the Lady Alice Tyrell dated 1422. The church, falling into disrepair, was saved by the All Saints' Society and is now in the care of the Redundant Churches Fund and holds concerts throughout the summer on Saturdays where artists give their services free.

In the woods surrounding Thorndon Hall is a chantry chapel, erected in 1870. In it was re-interred, on 16th October 1874, the remains of the executed Earl of Derwentwater. James, 3rd and last Earl of Derwentwater, having been taken prisoner after the battle of Preston when the Jacobite army was defeated in 1715, was beheaded on Tower Hill on 24th February 1716.

Dr Earle of Brentwood, medical man to Lord Petre, was present when the coffin was opened for identification. His daughter later described the scene: 'The body was in three coffins, first an oak one. Then one covered with crimson velvet and then a leaden one. When the lid of this was raised they looked on the perfect face and figure of a young and very handsome man fully dressed with a lace cravat bound tightly round his neck. And even as they looked he was not, face and figure faded from before their eyes and in its place a skeleton, the air had done its work, and they asked each other had they really seen this very man, dead for over 150 years. The next day he was laid to rest in the chantry chapel'.

Kelvedon Hatch ✒

Kelvedon Hatch lies between Brentwood High Street and Ongar. The village may perhaps not seem to be worth a second glance when driving through and yet it has quite a story to tell. Take 'Brizes' for instance, a mansion house standing on a small estate and seen from the main road. A medieval house once stood in these grounds, built by Thomas Bryce, a dealer in fabrics in 1498. The house was named Bryce. The existing mansion was built in 1720. In 1882 Bryce was held by a Mr Royd. A certain gentleman, Mr Randall, went shooting one day and shot a pheasant on Mr Royd's land, who went so far as to bring the gentleman to court to fine him. Mr Randall was so angered at being brought to court and declared he owed Mr Royd a grudge. In 1906 he built a row of cottages, placing them in full view of the Manor so that they caused a blot on the otherwise open landscape. To this day they are known as the IOU's.

The name Bryce was changed to Brizes and later owned by the Hon Simon Rodney, a descendant of a distinguished family line dating from 1140. He was also a cousin of Winston Churchill. His parents were friends of Sir William Baden Powell who, when he was forming the idea of a scouting movement asked permission to borrow Simon Rodney and his three brothers. He took them away and taught them the art of camping out. The Hon Simon Rodney was always proud to boast that he was the first ever Boy Scout. After his death Brizes was sold and is now a private boarding and day school named the Bell House School

The village can boast of another mansion, a rather imposing entrance gate with a lodge either side is the entrance to the Kelvedon Hall estate. A long driveway leads to a stately mansion built in three sections and set in extensive grounds. A certain John Wright possessed the estate in 1538. Kelvedon Hall was held by his descendants for nearly four centuries and there were ten successive John Wrights. The eighth John Wright entirely rebuilt the Hall which has remained unchanged to this day. In 1836 a member of the family, Samuel Wright, emigrated to America where he became the ancestor of Wilbur and Orwell Wright, pioneers of the aeroplane. There are Americans who bear the name of Wright and make a point of visiting Kelvedon Hall as the home of their ancestor!

There was no day schooling recorded in the village, but during 1812–16 the rector taught reading to 30 children on Sundays. A kindly lady also gave lessons. A school was built and opened in 1898. The building contained two classrooms and the schoolhouse which still remains. Because of the increase in population a modern school was built in the grounds behind the old school and was opened in 1968.

Gas did not come into the village until 1955 and electricity much later. Employment was once found on the local farms, which all had their own farmers, and on the staff of the manor houses. Today most of the villagers commute to the city.

Langdon Hills ✿

Langenduna (long hill) is recorded in Domesday Book as consisting of one manor held by Suene of Essex while adjacent Leindune (Laindon) took its name from a stream called the Lyge rising near St Nicholas' church. Between the two stood Leam (Westle and Eastle) held by the Canons of St Paul's. Records here are confusing and in 1432 Eastle was combined with Laindon and Westle with Langdon.

There are no very old buildings left in the area. A house still stands on the site of Westle manor which had belonged previously to Edith, Queen of Edward the Confessor and there are timbers in a barn reputedly from the original house. Hall Farm now stands on the site of the manor of Langdon and Goldsmiths, once a farm in the parish of Horndon-on-the-Hill and ceded to Langdon at some unknown date, has been much altered over the years. All three are now private dwellings.

The old church was built in the 16th century but traces in the walls suggest that it was the site of an older building. Standing at the entrance to Hall Farm, it is reasonable to suppose that this was the original church of which there seems to be no records. This church has now been declared redundant and has been converted to a private dwelling.

The new church was built in 1876 on top of the hill, an impressive building backed by beautiful woods. Opposite stands the old schoolhouse. Many of the older houses, particularly farms, have been swallowed up by the encroachment of Basildon new town and only their names remain as a reminder of the past.

In 1588 a beacon was erected on top of the hill as part of a warning system when a Spanish invasion seemed imminent. This was rebuilt in 1803 when a French invasion was feared and the field at the corner of Dry Street on top of the hill still carries the name Beacon Field.

The bulk of the residential part of Langdon Hills developed after the coming of the railway. A number of big family houses were built along the road leading from the station to The Crown on top of the hill and these were interspersed with smaller houses and bungalows, some in side roads leading off the High Road. Today most residents commute to London or work in Thameside industries.

Langham

Langham is a long parish, with St Mary's church, old and small, very pleasantly situated among woods on high ground overlooking the valley of the river Stour. Constable's Cottage, near the church, recalls the work of John Constable, whose home in East Bergholt was not many miles away. He learned to love the lanes through the parish and especially the paths through Langham Hall woods down into the river valley and to Stratford St Mary. He liked to amble along absorbing the country life about him.

When Dr Fisher, rector of Langham in 1799, became Bishop of Salisbury, he installed his nephew, John Fisher, as curate in charge at Langham rectory. John Fisher became a firm friend of John Constable and helped the artist in the courtship of his beloved Maria, againnst strong family opposition. Thus Langham rectory became the romantic scene of clandestine meetings between the lovers. So Constable had a double reason for loving Langham. From the woods of Langham Hall, he painted his famous *Dedham Vale*, and about the same time he made several sketches of 'a cottage scene with Langham church'. Years later, from these sketches, he painted the lovely *Glebe Farm*, now in the Tate Gallery.

In the early 1950s, Mr George Dummer planted a chance apple seedling in his back garden. It turned out to be a most delicious early apple, soon to be known as *Dummer's Pride*. When the Press got wind of this new variety, together with the great interest and excitement created by the fruit-growers and nurserymen, they wrote about the new discovery. The apple quickly put Langham on the map. However, supposedly for commercial reasons, the new apple was re-named *Discovery* in 1961. One of the Langham fruit farms can now boast the oldest *Discovery* orchard in the world. Slowly but surely the apple has grown in popularity so that it is almost equal to a *Worcester*.

A lady from Langham's history emerged from the Victoria and Albert Museum to make an appearance at the Age of Chivalry exhibition in 1987. Described as 'a rare survival', and beautiful though damaged, she was a Virgin with the Child on her knee, dated about 1220, about 15″ tall, sculptured in oak and with traces of the bright pigments which once decorated the figures still to be detected in the Romanesque draperies. The sculpture used to be in Langham church, probably as an altar piece.

Langley 🐝

Langley is a small village of about 500 people. There are two distinct parts of Langley, Upper and Lower Greens. Upper Green is high and breezy, almost the highest point in Essex, nearly 500 feet above sea level. Lower Green is more sheltered along the valley of the Stort, here only a small stream.

'Langley' means long lea or pasture. According to local tradition cattle and horses on their way to market from the north were put to graze in the rich meadows by the meanderings of the stream. The only surviving pub in Langley, the Bull, on Lower Green must always have been prosperous from the drovers and graziers congregating there. Opposite the Bull the cottage which was once used for the Langley poor still has on its wall the constable's warning that beggars will be whipped.

Up the lane from the Bull, near Upper Green, are the parish church and the ancient manor house. From the churchyard the wide views into Essex, Hertfordshire and Cambridgeshire, are of big arable fields, but still with patches of woodland, tucked-away cottages and isolated farms. The fields each side of Bull Lane have always been enormous. Until the mid 19th century they were the two great open fields of Langley, North field and Peaseland field, divided into innumerable strips with pathways in between. The view to the west beyond Lower Green to Langley Lawn Farm would, in the Middle Ages, have shown a great enclosed park for hunting and until the Second World War it was all rough grazing and woodland. Now it is all arable, but deer still live in the remaining pockets of woodland round Langley.

The church is very small but beautiful, with its Norman porch, Norman and 14th century windows, 15th century hammerbeam roof and brickbuilt chancel with the Stuart coat of arms in the east window. Next to the church there has been a manor house, Langley Hall, since the Middle Ages, when part of Langley was made into a separate manor from the much bigger manor of Clavering, and given to the priory of St Bartholomew, Smithfield, London. Today Langley Hall is a stout 17th century farmhouse. In front of it the ample yard and outbuildings include an 18th century dovecote and at the entrance is a big duck pond. It is still a working farm. Surely this is one of the most picturesque views in Essex.

In the early 19th century Langley was famous for its poachers. Several were transported to Botany Bay in 1829 after a foray with gamekeepers, one of whom was killed.

Langley cricketers were flourishing in the 19th century and they have gone on to acquire fame beyond Essex, reaching the final stages in national village cricket competitions. Fielding may be hazardous because the pitch on Upper Green is bisected by the road to Duddenhoe End, but the turf has always been first class. The old men used to complain that they could not find a bent to clean their pipes when they came to watch.

The Lavers

The three villages which comprise the Lavers lie to the north-west of Ongar, on high ground which is well drained by many streams. This accounts for the name Laver, derived from an Old English word meaning 'stream passage'. It is a rural area and the main industry is farming which is evident from the well maintained farms throughout the area.

Each of the three villages, High, Little and Magdalen Laver

retains its own identity and parish church, although they share the same rector and are united in many ways.

To the east lies Little Laver, one of the smallest villages in the neighbourhood. There were only 15 inhabited houses in 1801 and the current electoral register lists only 78 souls. The church, rebuilt in the 14th century, was added to in Victorian times and stands in the grounds of the old manor house.

In the north is High Laver where in the 18th century the philosopher John Locke spent the last years of his life with the Masham family at Otes, a red bricked Tudor manor house. He lived there from 1691 until his death in 1704. He is buried in High Laver churchyard, having written his own epitaph which is now inside the 12th century church on the south wall.

An interesting listed building is Mashams, a 14th century hall house, very little altered through the years, and which, on the death of its owner, will be left to the Passmore Edwards Museum Trust to be used as a 'living museum'. Each year a garden party is held in its grounds for the Lavers residents, raising money for local charities.

Magdalen Laver lies to the south and is a parish of scattered houses with an unusual number of ancient timber framed farmhouses, many of which stand on or near moated sites. One of the most attractive of these is Bushes, a 15th century farmhouse.

The parish church of St Mary Magdalen is most picturesque, constructed in the 12th century with a 16th century wooden tower. It stands, almost hidden, in a field near the manor house, approached by a tree-lined chase, although prior to the Second World War it could only be reached via footpaths. A former rector was William Webb Ellis who, whilst at Rugby school, picked up the ball during a football game and ran with it, thereby establishing the game of Rugby Football. He also founded the village school in 1862, this was closed in 1960.

To the north of the church is Pole Lane, an ancient byway reputed to be the main street of the medieval village, deserted at the time of the Black Death.

In the three Lavers villages there are now only two public houses, the Green Man in Magdalen Laver and the John Barleycorn in High Laver. There are no post offices and the village shop closed in 1969. This would seem to indicate a dying community but this is not so. The village hall in Magdalen Laver, although isolated, serves as a centre for all the Lavers and is in constant use. There is also a flourishing Horticultural Society which, although only a few years old, secured a Gold Medal at Chelsea Flower Show at their first attempt.

Layer de la Haye

Leire, thought to be the origin of the Layer Brook was mentioned in the Domesday Book. The name of de la Haye (of Norman origin) was first recorded in the Charter of the Benedictine Abbey of St John in Colchester dated 1128. The main road may have been one of the main routes the Roman soldiers took to reach the river Blackwater which can be seen from the church, and the North Sea is but four to five miles distant as the seagull flies. On the boundaries lies the bird sanctuary and the reservoir.

Some of the place-names speak for themselves. The Roman river. The Charity Wood, apparently so-called because the firewood for the poor was cut from it. Cheste Wood, meaning 'strife'. The Kiln, where a medieval tile kiln was unearthed years ago. A Belgic ditch was discovered which was used in the defence of Camulodunum. Malting Green where the maltings were, and a tollgate was sited nearby. 'Blind Knights' was a hospital during the Crusades.

The village is well sought-after. Artists enjoy and paint the many old houses and beauty spots. Many professional people choose to live here, its peaceful surroundings and convenience to the town and sea, add to its charm. The addition of the private estate in the centre in no way spoils its attractions, indeed it not only adds to the population but makes for a well-balanced community.

There are industries – the Anglian Waterworks have their pumping station here; the Kiln has a thriving saddlery business, and the mill runs a successful mushroom farm. There are builders and decorators, electricians, plumbers, hairdressers, video servicer and a picture framer! A post office, and two shops, seem to provide all our needs, and a garage.

Little Baddow 🌿

Tofts manor house was named after William Toft who died in 1470. The builder and first resident of the present white brick house was a brother of the first Lord Rayleigh. He was Major General William Gooday Strutt (1762–1848) after whom the General Arms public house is named.

Little Baddow mill, on the banks of the Chelmer beside the road to Boreham, is mentioned in the Domesday Book but another mill which existed at the bottom of North Hill in the 1330s was used to make paper in the 18th century.

The church of St Mary the Virgin dates from Norman times and inside are two extremely rare 14th century wooden effigies, thought to be of Sir John and Lady Filiol (after whom Phillows Farm is called). The large 14th century wall painting of St Christopher was uncovered in 1922 by the rector, the Reverend (later Canon) Jesse Berridge, author of books based on Little Baddow.

Old Riffhams, originally built by Richer de Rifham in 1308, has a rare Sun Insurance firemark over the door. The building was refaced in brick in the 18th century. The Woolley family lived there in 1915 and their son, Sir Leonard Woolley the archaeologist carried out a scientific excavation of the city of Ur of the Chaldees.

The adjoining woodland, medieval Blakes Wood now owned by the National Trust, is renowned as one of the most beautiful bluebell woods in Essex. It was named after its 16th century owners, the Blake family, whose descendants went to New England in 1635. Before Richard Blake built New Bassetts in the late 1700s the family lived in the timber farmhouse Old Bassetts.

Cukoos Farm was where non-conformists worshipped led by Thomas Hooker, who had been banned from preaching in Chelmsford. His assistant John Eliot went to America in 1631, became apostle to the Indians, and made the first translation of the Bible into Algonquin Indian. Thomas Hooker went first to Holland and then to America, where in 1636 he helped found the State of Connecticut, providing the USA's first written constitution. Two commemorative plaques were unveiled in 1986, one at Cukoos and the other beside Chelmsford Cathedral.

The United Reformed church was built in 1708 and pastor from 1780 to 1799 was the Reverend William Parry who helped found the Essex Congregational Union.

Little Baddow Hall, originally the Norman manor house of Beadewan, now has 14th century timbers. Stuart Macdonald transformed its fields into apple orchards in 1928.

Little Clacton

Little Clacton is a pleasant and popular place to live and has a steady increase in population.

The Blacksmith's Arms still stands in sight of the church but the forge and a group of old houses are now replaced with a modern garage. This inn is at least 200 years old and the open space in front of it was once the site of an annual fair held to celebrate St James' Day. In 1806 the Blacksmith's Arms was the setting for a fight between villagers and some of the Cameron Highlanders who were stationed at nearby Weeley. The men of Little Clacton chased the soldiers along the street until one, Alexander McDonald, who had hurt his foot, was struck down and died. Legend says that where his head hit the roadside a hole appeared which resisted all efforts to fill it. The event is recorded on a tombstone in Weeley churchyard where the soldier was buried.

The church of St James the Great dates mostly from the 14th century but the chancel, which has a Norman window and priest's door, is thought to be 12th century. The font dates from 1190 and one of the three bells housed in the wooden turret was cast by Robert Crouch in 1437. This is thought to be the only one of his bells to remain in Essex.

In 1596 William Hubbard who lived at Bovills Hall left £100 14s to be used as a charity fund for the poor of the village. A farm was bought at St Osyth Heath and although sold in 1944 the profit was invested by the trustees and the income is still distributed at Christmas time. There is a brass on the wall of the church in memory of William and three of his four wives!

Most of the people in old Little Clacton were farm workers and worried that the introduction of machinery would put them out of a job. In 1830 a group of them marched to the Lodge Farm where a thrashing machine was kept, broke into the barn and smashed the machine to pieces.

Little Waltham 🦌

'So silently they one to th'other come,
As colours steal into the pear or plum,
And air-like, leave no pression to be seen
Where e're they met, or parting place has been'.
                                        Robert Herrick.

However secret the meeting place, someone knew where they met,
those lovers, and the story has passed down through the generations of Little Waltham villagers for 450 years.

What was Little Waltham like in those days? St Martin's church
was there of course, though smaller than today, and one of the
Mildmay family lived at the old hall which then stood between the
lake and the modern Pond House. Some of the very old houses in
the village may have been standing at that time, and most of the
farms, Pratts, Longs, Powers, Belsteads and Channells amongst
others. There was some arable land, but a lot more grass than
there is now and there were many acres of woods and gorsy
heathland.

In 1517 Sir Thomas Boleyn, father of the famous Anne, gave to
Henry VIII his house called New Hall in Boreham. The house was
rebuilt in the next years. Henry was very well-pleased with New
Hall and renamed it Beaulieu. The people of Little Waltham must
have been in contact with all this. Park Farm, at that time called
New Lodge, was within the Park of New Hall, and the tenant had
to carry loads of straw to New Hall as part of his service.

At that time, one of the park-keepers or wardens lived in Little
Waltham at a cottage on Blasford Hill. The building is still there,
on the left as you go to Chelmsford and was once, possibly, the old
manor of Blastard's Fee. It is very old and has a thatched roof.
This is where Henry VIII and the young Anne Boleyn used to meet
in secret, arriving it is said, from different directions, to avoid
suspicion!

A very different story about Little Waltham comes from the
1930s. What on earth is a Flapping Track? The track, or stadium
was, in fact, announced on a large board erected next to the Little
Waltham Garage – 'The Waltham Greyhound and Whippet Racing Club'. Flapping meant that it was un-licensed. It was one of

many such tracks that sprang up locally in the 1930s. Others were at Braintree, Thaxted, Stondon Massey and on the King's Head meadow in Chelmsford.

The track was started in 1930 by Bill Cass who owned the Little Waltham Garage with the land behind, and by Frank Stewart, builder of Roman Road and Manor Crescent. The grass track or stadium covered the whole area of land which is now occupied by the Chelmer Avenue houses and gardens.

The track closed down about 1938. After the Second World War there were requests to start the racing again, but the Parish Council did not give permission for this to happen and a few years later the land was built over.

Manningtree ❧

Manningtree owes its importance to the river Stour. It lies at the head of the estuary, nine miles west of Harwich. Bronze Age men sailed up and down the river 4000 years ago to trade and traces of settlements have been found in the area, in the form of arrow heads, spear heads etc. It is probable that Roman ships called here, or at Mistley, with cargoes for Colchester. Saxons settled here, and Vikings raided Brantham, across the river in Suffolk. William the Conqueror handed over the manor to his half sister, the Countess of Aumale (Albemarle) as a reward for her help.

The old manor house of Schiddingchou has long since disappeared and local people are prepared to argue over the site it occupied. Medieval, Tudor, Georgian, Victorian and modern houses rub shoulders in the present community.

The railway reached the area in 1846. Manningtree station was built at the junction of roads from Harwich, Colchester and Ipswich, in Lawford on an embankment made with soil taken from cuttings at Mistley!

A strange story from the beginning of this century concerned Dame Maurus, the nun who found freedom at Manningtree. Margaret Moult, at the age of 16, had decided to become a nun and had entered the closed Benedictine order at the Abbey of St Mary, East Bergholt, Suffolk. After four years she tried to leave but it was to be seven years after entering the order that she finally slipped away. Pursued, she found sanctuary at Manningtree railway station before returning to her family in London. Presentations to the railwaymen who had helped her were made by the Protestant Alliance.

Manuden 🌿

Manuden, or 'common valley', was an established village community at the time of the Domesday survey when it was known as Magghedana, one of over 40 variants. The tiny village of only 200 houses nestles in a valley, four miles north of Bishop's Stortford, where its picturesque thatched cottages and timbered buildings hug the main street which meanders through the village almost parallel with the river. Although for centuries unchanged, the last 100 years has seen Manuden transformed from a sleepy, Essex village dependent upon agriculture, into a haven for commuters.

The large houses like Manuden Hall and Manuden House with their once large staffs of servants, cooks and grooms belong to a past era, although there are still villagers who can remember their heyday. Gone too is the mill, the maltings and the whitening manufacturer, all employers in their time.

The advent of the family car and close proximity of supermarkets in nearby Bishop's Stortford and Saffron Walden has made the village shop redundant. The post office no longer acts as a general store but hires out videos, a sure sign of the changing times. Older residents can remember two provisions shops, a bakery, a teashop and a funeral service as well as cobblers and tailors. Today there is only one shop selling local crafts and clothes, plus a garage, appropriately enough on the site of what was once the local smithy and wheelwright.

Occupying a central position in the village is the stone and flint church of St Mary, officially dated from 1143 but largely medieval and much rebuilt between 1863–67. It contains a magnificent, early 15th century, carved oak choir screen, complete with little green men, and a splendid pipe organ given by Rev J. B. Forster in 1912. On the north wall of the vestry an impressive wall tablet commemorates Sir William Waad, a notable diplomat and Officer of State to Elizabeth I and James I, and who as eight year Lieutenant of The Tower of London was custodian of Guy Fawkes and Sir Walter Raleigh. Sir William's residence was Battles Hall,

1½ miles north west of the village where his grandson Capt William Waad was brutally murdered in 1677. The assassin was later executed in Chelmsford but Richard Savill, who robbed and killed villager Thomas Bray in 1789 suffered hanging on Manuden Downs facing his mother's cottage.

In common with other villages Manuden's clergy and parishioners suffered persecution throughout history. In March 1431 vicar Thomas Bagley was burnt at the stake in Smithfield for heresy. Two hundred years later Thomas Crowley of Manuden Hall was being persecuted for his Catholic belief. However, this good man obviously forgave his tormentors as he bequeathed a charity to the poor of Manuden which, along with several others, is still administered today.

Manuden may be a commuter village but it is certainly not a 'dormitory'. Much goes on here. The Village Hall, once a Congregational Chapel, is fully booked as a meeting place for many groups. This is not a pretty museum piece but a lively community.

The Maplesteads ✺

The Maplesteads are villages off the beaten track. People come to visit of course and it has been known for some to enter and leave without even being aware they had been on target for their visit.

One well known local character was Miss Pratt. Miss Alice Pratt was born in Great Maplestead and lived her long life in the village. She was nanny to the children of Dynes Hall, a lovely Queen Anne house well worth a visit when the gardens are open for charity events. When her nannying days were over and later in life she ran the village post office and shop. Those who remember can vouch for the fact that she would come into the shop from blackleading the grate to fulfil your request for sweets or biscuits by plunging her hands into the tins and jars. The perfume on the goods was strongly of paraffin or blacklead or whatever chore was in process at the time. Miss Pratt, who by this time was getting on in years, was a lively lady who was the living image of Giles' Grandma, flat black straw hat, straight black coat, well down towards her ankles and black flat heeled shoes.

At Little Maplestead there is the very beautiful Round Church built by the Knights Hospitallers of St John. It has a circular plan and is one of the four Round Churches in England of this design. In June each year on St John the Baptist Day a service is held to which the leaders of the Order come dressed in full regalia. Together with members of the St John's Ambulance Brigade there is a procession after the service which attracts not a few sightseers.

The House of Mercy, built in 1867, now sadly no longer in existence, was run by the Clewer Sisters for 'wayward girls'. The Rev Mylrea was warden just prior to the Second World War. Mrs Mylrea was attending a service in the private chapel of the home when she saw a nun standing behind her husband at the altar. Later she asked him who it was and why she was there. It appeared that no one else had seen this nun.

Marks Tey ✣

In Saxon times, Marks Tey was owned by Uleric. Geoffrey de Mandeville later had Marks Tey, which was then called Tey Mandeville. Later on, the village was rented to a family from Calais, called de Merk, hence Marks Tey. It has also been called Tey ad Ulmos (Tey with the elms), and there is an Elm Lane in the village. Sadly, like everywhere else, the elms have gone.

Marks Tey's main importance was as somewhere to go through on the way to somewhere else! The road between Marks Tey and Colchester was turnpiked in 1694, between Marks Tey and Chelmsford in 1726, and between Marks Tey and Braintree in 1765. This resulted in an improvement in transport by road and the inns flourished.

Situated between Colchester and Coggeshall, which were both major wool towns, Marks Tey was bound to be involved in the wool trade in some way. There were almost certainly outworkers here, but Marks Tey's main contribution was in the growing of teasels. These were used during the finishing process, after fulling, when the shearmen would bring up the nap using teasels, before clipping it off neatly. They were grown where the present playing field is now situated, and the odd wild teasel can still be found growing there.

During the Civil War, there was a famous Siege of Colchester. On successive days the Royalist armies and the Cromwellian armies each marched through Marks Tey. It is reputed that due to its being in the line of fire, the church tower was hit by an errant cannon ball. The tower had to be demolished, but as funds could not stretch to providing stone, it had to be rebuilt in wood. This has provided Marks Tey with a very interesting church tower, clad with wooden shingles.

In recent years, Marks Tey has expanded its population due to the building of housing estates within walking distance of the station. For this reason, many of the inhabitants are commuters. Local businesses such as the brickworks at Marks Tey are also employers.

Matching 🌿

The original site of the village was at Church Green. After the 5th century the community spread to form two villages – Matching Green and Matching Tye – and three hamlets, Newmans End, Housham Tye and Carters Green.

The names Tye and Green are reminders of the clearings cut in the forest, the winding woodland paths giving their name to Tye, literally a knot or cross-road, and Green which is a clearing in the forest.

By the time of the Norman Conquest there were many manors in the parish, of which three remain – Matching Hall, Housham (formerly Ovesham) Hall and Stock Hall.

Until the early 20th century, Matching people experienced near-primitive conditions by present standards – no water or electricity and very low wages. Except at harvest time, few women worked and their menfolk were labourers on the many farms, or walked three miles to Moreton Mill.

There were shops around Matching Green (none now) – a cycle agent, a saddlery/shoe shop, a forge, a draper, a grocer, a bakery, two butchers and a maltings with oast house and kiln. At one time there were six public houses! One remains, The Chequers, and has been trading for as long as anyone can remember.

In 1886 the village school was built but prior to this there was a penny school (now Green Edge Cottage) which, as the name suggests, required pupils to pay teacher one penny per week.

During the Second World War, farm land was requisitioned and an arifield built by the Americans for the 391st Bomber Group of the US 9th Airforce. Most of the land used for this airfield has been reclaimed but the Control Tower remains and the radar is still used by Cossers of Harlow for testing equipment.

One resident of Matching Green was Augustus John, the artist. He lived at Elm House, next to The Chequers, with his wife, children and mistress. One elderly lady still living in the village, recalls he was disliked because he painted nude ladies, which was definitely 'not done in those days'.

Mention must be made of the Marriage Feast Room. It stands at the west end of the church and is said to have been built by William Chimney (about 1480) for use of local brides for their wedding breakfast. It was last used for this purpose in 1936 but the privilege remains. In the 18th century it was used as an almshouse, and, more recently has provided living accommodation for the church organist. Today it is used for church functions.

The spread parish of Matching has of course seen changes, but today Church Green remains virtually as it was at the time of the Saxon settlement. The lovely church of St Mary the Virgin stands on the site of the original wooden church, the ancient Marriage Feast Room to its west, and Matching Hall on the other side of the Green. It is an idyllic spot.

Mayland 🌿

Mayland is a widely spread community of which the larger part by far lies along the southern shore of the river Blackwater. This area is known as Maylandsea, as distinct from Mayland proper which consists of scattered houses spread over Mayland Hill to the south.

Mayland was originally a manor dating from the 12th century, when it formed part of the endowment of St Osyth's priory. In the time of Henry VIII it was bestowed on Cardinal Wolsey, until his fall from grace, and then passed through various hands, until in the 18th century it was acquired by St Bartholomew's Hospital. They it was who built the present church of St Barnabas in 1866, after an earlier church had fallen into decay.

This early history may explain why Mayland has no visible ancient centre. Within almost living memory the community consisted of a few scattered farms: Parsonage Farm, high on the hill, with the benefit of the church close by, Marsh Farm and Nipsells

Farm, down by the lonely Blackwater estuary. In the midst of them stood a windmill, long since demolished, which is commemorated in the name of the Mayland Mill public house. The Mill House still stands, in its garden a large rockery reputedly built with stones from the old mill.

In the early years of the present century Mayland might well have become a model co-operative agricultural community. A certain Mr Fels, an American who had made a vast fortune from Naphtha Soap, sought to do something for the exploited working class of the East End of London. Mayland seemed the ideal spot to establish two rows of smallholdings. The venture foundered when the ground proved unsuitable for intensive cultivation and the smallholders discovered they could earn more by working for someone else. A few of the original homesteads still remain.

Another phase in the chequered history of Mayland came with the establishment of Cardnells Boatyard, where boats of all varieties were built and repairs carried out, including the refitting of lifeboats. In the Second World War the yard employed between 80 and 90 men turning out motor torpedo boats for the Admiralty. Since then Maylandsea has blossomed into a sizeable sailing centre, with imposing clubhouses and a forest of dinghies, some hauled up on the riverbank, others at anchor in the creek.

Between the wars Mayland had been 'discovered' by Londoners seeking a retreat where they could build, usually with their own hands, a chalet or bungalow in which to spend weekends and holidays. After the Second World War the community grew apace, but it was still largely a holiday and retirement area, until the developers arrived, buying up the old plots and finding room for several houses where once a tiny shack had stood. There are now over 2000 names on the electoral roll.

Moreton

Moreton is an attractive village situated to the north of the A414 between Epping and Ongar. The name implies that there was a settlement here in Saxon times and indeed, in 1039 the church was presented to the monastery of St Albans by the lord of the manor. The present church was built on the same site in the 13th century, with the tower added in the 16th or 17th century.

Many of the buildings date back to the 15th or 16th century including one of the two public houses, The White Hart. The other, situated opposite, is The Moreton Massey (formerly The Nag's Head) and this is 18th century. These two hostelries enjoy a friendly rivalry which is manifested each Boxing Day, since 1969, when a team from each competes in obstacle races and other games in the main street, culminating in a tug-of-war across Cripsey Brook, the losers finishing rather wet! This draws many hundreds of spectators from whom a collection is taken for a local charity.

Another interesting building is a timber framed 15th century hall cottage, built as a Guildhall in 1473 for the Guild of All Saints which paid 4/4d annually to the rector for masses to be said for the souls of the deceased guildmen. It is now called Black Hall.

Although the main industry in the area is farming, other local industries play an important part in village life. The first of these is the extraction of gravel from a pit within the village boundaries which is of significant economic importance, and was originally owned by a prominent village family. The second industry involving many local people is the mill. Originally there was a postmill, erected about 1715, and in constant use until 1931. Gradually the mill fell into disrepair and was finally demolished in 1964. However, the site is still used as a mill and a few years ago was sold to Dalgety Spillers.

At one end of the village street there is an old First World War hangar in which several traction engines are housed. These were used for threshing until modern farming methods took over. In the 1920s the teams of men who travelled around the farms at threshing time were so unruly that the village policeman had to carry a revolver to deal with the fights that occurred.

All these industries were, and in many cases still are, owned by local people whose families go back many generations. This, together with the fact that the main buildings including the church, manor house, school, village hall, public houses, post office, and until recently, the village shop, are all situated within a ¼ mile of each other has resulted in a close-knit community where everyone works together.

Mountnessing ✑

Time was when the traveller from East Anglia to London recognised the approach of this village by its most obvious landmark, the windmill, standing high at the crossroads in the centre of the village to catch the prevailing westerly winds. Today's traveller passes at high speed by train or along the A12 by-pass.

The existence of a mill on this spot can be traced back to at least 1580. The structure you can see today is the restored postmill constructed in about 1807. In 1937 the mill was taken over by the Parish Council and the site was given to the parish by Lord Arran, the then owner of Thoby Hall. Restoration was completed in 1983 by the county millwright and the mill is now regularly open to the public during the summer.

Thoby Hall was built on the site of Thoby Priory, the home of the canons of St Augustine. Their first prior was Tobias and the charter, which dates from about 1151, was witnessed not only by Michael de Capra their founder but by Robert de Mountney. The 'lands of the Mountneys', is modernised as Mountnessing.

It is likely that Robert de Mountney lived at Mountnessing Hall, an imposing manor, some two miles from the centre of the village standing adjacent to the village church dedicated to St Giles, patron saint of beggars and cripples. The church dates from Norman times having evidence of puddingstone in its walls. There are two explanations to consider for the remoteness of this church. The hamlet may have existed around the church and hall and subsequently disappeared, alternatively the church may have been the private chapel of the manor. The latter gains credence as there was a small door in the north wall, now bricked up, which was most likely the entrance for the lord of the manor. The most interesting feature of the church is perhaps the tower, supported by huge wooden beams.

The village of 100 years ago was based on agriculture but today's inhabitants are commuters to neighbouring Brentwood and the capital. Notwithstanding this the same community spirit exists. In 1977 following the successful Silver Jubilee celebrations the committee responsible set their talents to work to build a village hall. This was opened in 1985 and fulfils its purpose in providing a focal point for village activities. Conveniently it is set

Mountnessing Windmill

adjacent to a recreation field, tennis courts and the windmill, whilst across the road is the Prince of Wales, one of three public houses in the village. The others are the Plough almost next door and the George and Dragon some way towards Brentwood along Roman Road, a rightly named thoroughfare, straight as a die through the village.

Mundon

The settlement here was called Munduna, a 'defensive mound', a name given by its Saxon invaders. They recognised the natural defensive position and enhanced it by constructing their own moated enclosure. It became a thriving settlement.

The building of a small parish church was begun in the 13th century with a timber framed semi-octagonal belfry added 400 years later. The church was part of the Abbey of St John in Colchester and the chantry land included the land of Iltney Farm.

Richard Solly in the early 1800s came to the hall built close to the church and began to improve the land. Solly planted a wood to the south of the ancient oak grove first known as 'the plantation' and then as 'the herony' when herons migrated from a wood near London.

A population of 287 souls in the middle of the 19th century spread the limits of the settlement to the west and south. A thriving country community supported a wheelwright, a boot and shoemaker, a blacksmith, a baker and shopkeeper, a curate, a parish clerk and a postmistress.

The village suffered a great deal from the depression of the 1930s and from enemy action during the Second World War. A village hall was constructed on land given by the then owner of the hall a little to the west of the church, a symbol of victory and continuity after the ravages of war. In the 1970s the Friends of Friendless Churches started to restore St Mary's to something of its former glory. Although the nave still remained unsafe in 1977 a christening took place in the large belfry. By 1985 the church was once more proud and full, if only infrequently.

Navestock 🦃

Navestock has a long history dating from Roman times and is mentioned in the Domesday Book as having three manors, woods sufficient to feed 900 pigs and four hives of bees.

Part of the old forest remains at Curtis Mill Green bounded by the M25 and by Richards Stone and Navestock Stone, two ancient stones marking the edge of the royal forest. In 1858 Curtis Mill Green was allotted as common to the villagers. Present day inhabitants have re-registered their rights to herbage, estovers and grazing. Water and electricity are available to most homes but oil lamps were the only light and water came from the public hand pump until well after the Second World War.

The parish church dating back to Norman times has many memorials including those to Elizabeth, daughter of the 3rd Earl Waldegrave and lady of the bedchamber to Queen Charlotte. The Waldegraves held the manor from 1554 and in 1776 enclosed Navestock common. Their 18th century mansion was demolished in 1811.

From 1900 – 1940 Navestock was still a village of country people. Five gamekeepers and 8 to 10 gardeners were employed on the estate. Roads were bad and often flooded. In those days the village had a baker. In Sabines Green a delicious smell of baking bread came from Mr Goodwin's bakery; later it became a post office.

During the time of cattle and grass the Essex Hunt had wonderful runs through Navestock. The Duchess of Sutherland, a well-known shot, would join the shoots on the estate. Point-to-point horses were kept at Navestock Hall. All these country sports continue with as much enjoyment as ever.

The church has survived all these changes including in 1644 the theft of some brasses, probably by Cromwell's soldiers. In 1940 a noise like a train came through the sky. The parachute of a land mine became entangled in the churchyard trees and the mine exploded. The tower timbers withstood the blast.

Many Navestock people work outside the village but five farmers remain. The four public houses cater for all, serving pub lunches to an increasing numbers of visitors. Above everything is the steady drone of the traffic on the M25.

Nazeing 🌿

The parish church of All Saints is an ancient building sited on a headland overlooking the Lee valley. Hence the name of Nazeing, originally Nazinga, meaning headland and meadow.

Proceeding along the lane to Nazeing common, one passes several cottages and the old post office, all listed as Grade II buildings. Lodge Farm standing remotely on the edge of the common dates from 1777. Legend has it that Boadicea, in approximately AD 61, drove her chariot down the common to be massacred, with 80,000 men, by the Romans.

In the Domesday Book, the common is mentioned as part of the Waltham Hundred, and was disafforested in 1285 for the men of Nazeing to have the rights of pasture. An Act of 1657 gave use of the land to the tenants of 101 ancient houses. This was further regulated in 1778. In the Second World War, the land was ploughed for food and a further Act of 1947 allowed the copyholders to let the land for farming. Thus, the Nazeing common is *not* a common, but private property, through which a public highway runs, and the correct name is Nazeing wood or park.

As the village is five miles long, it is divided into Upper Nazeing, Middle Street and Lower Nazeing. In Middle Street, at Nazeingbury, ancient crossroads bisect the village where, in 1404, stood the Bury Cross. The present house of 'Nazeingbury' dates back to Tudor times; in fact it was the home of Katherine Parr, the sixth wife of Henry VIII. The present occupiers, a doctor and his wife, declare that in one attic bedroom, in a cupboard, there is often a heavy scent of musk, and it is rumoured a legendary ghostly lady.

The affix 'bury' to Nazeingbury, applied to the communal graves dug to contain the bodies of plague victims, brought down by river barges from London. This area seems to be the extent of the funeral journeys, as graves were also dug at Broxbournebury and Wormleybury, within the district.

Down by the river Lee or Lea, at the turn of the century, the glasshouse industry was established, as the river valley soil was good and there was plentiful spring water. So tomatoes, grapes and cucumbers were grown and the produce taken overnight to Covent Garden by horse and cart. This industry attracted many Dutch, Danish and Norwegian immigrants and their surnames are now part of our heritage. This industry was at its height in the 1950s, but declined with the importation of cheap foreign fruit and the soaring price of oil needed to maintain the high temperatures. It revived partially in the 1970s, due to another group of immigrants – Italians. One famous name became a household word from this industry – Thomas Rochford's house plants. He also has closed down now.

Today, the Lee Valley Regional Park Authority is developing the derelict banks of the river by transforming them into parks and leisure centres, marinas and picnic areas. Just before Nazeing changes county and crosses the railway line, a Lido has appeared. There are small parks at Dobbs Weir, Broxbourne Meadow and the Waltham Abbey Gardens, under the shadow of the abbey walls.

In contrast, a relic of 'Harold's bridge' within the gardens is a last reminder of that ancient way the pilgrims walked from Epping Upland to give thanks in that great abbey, built by William I to commemorate the Conquest of England.

Nevendon ✣

Nevendon has had many different spellings of its name throughout its long history which dates back to Saxon times. Neutenden and Nezenden were two of these, and in the reign of Edward the Confessor it was called Newenden.

Cranes Farm and Cranes Farm Road owe the origin of their names to the Hugh Le Crane family that farmed it in 1272. Apparently the family of Sandell lived there in the 16th and 17th centuries. William Sandell in his will dated 1542 left bread and cheese and 20 shillings as alms for the poor at his burial and for a month after.

William and Thomas Austen are supposed to have lived at Framptons Farm, about 1653, and they are said to have been amongst those that endorsed the indictment of Mary Hurst for witchcraft. She was accused of bewitching William Hodge who was 'wasted and consumed' on 24th May 1653.

Nevendon's church is dedicated to St Peter and it still retains its original lancet windows, the existing chancel walls being 13th century. Great Bromfords, (that also gives its name to a road nowadys) was a large house over 500 years old and said to have contained a priest's hiding place. It was the local meeting place of the hunt and at one time had a moat surrounding it. Unfortunately it was demolished in 1951 after being damaged by enemy action in the Second World War.

The Old Tithe Barn was·built in Nevendon somewhere about the 1500s, villagers took a part of their produce there, where it was collected for the lord of the manor as part of their dues that they had to pay to him.·A preservation order was asked for at one time on the the tithe barn, this was refused, but is now under re-examination. At one time it was used as a local school, possibly in the middle 1800s. The old school stood to the west of St Peter's church and was built in 1886 as a National school, it later became a private house and was finally demolished in 1972. In the 18th century Elizabeth Kirkham (who died in 1788) was mistress of Nevendon's school for 27 years, she is buried in the local church.

Nevendon is changing fast, new modern housing estates are being built, new roads being laid. So much of the land is fast becoming unrecognisable and Burnt Mills Industrial Estate is expanding over what used to be fields and woods.

Newport 🐘

The Domesday Book (1086) shows Newport as an agricultural community of some 200 people, centred on a royal estate. 'Port' at this time meant any market, even though it be inland, under the control of the King. This particular 'port' must have been 'new' sometime in the 10th century and perhaps was even created as one of a series of fortifications against the Danes. Like other fortified towns of the time, it has a triangular shaped village green, which is overlooked by the church.

How though did this triangular centre of the village get the extraordinary name 'Elephant Green'? The tale goes that one year a visiting circus passed this way and an elephant died as it crossed the green. One can imagine the problems and the excitement this event would cause, which would justify commemorating it down the years by naming the spot after it.

Newport has a large boulder, at its northern end by the side of the busy B1383, which is called locally the 'Leper Stone'. Here food was supposedly left for the sufferers, in the Middle Ages, who were lodged at St Leonard's Hospital nearby. Excavations for the new houses that stand on the site near the stone, did reveal human bones but although these were, thankfully, proved ancient, they did not show any signs of leprosy.

Near the centre of the village, in the High Street, stands a private house Monks Barn, which has an interesting ornamental carving of religious theme. The house is thought to have been given its name because it was once a resting place for travelling monks.

In 1692, the owners of the Crown House, in Bridge End, had their hostelry refronted the way it is today, with a crown design in the pargetting. However, the actual building is much older. Folk-lore has it that this was where, when Charles II stayed 'down the road' at Audley End House, he arranged for his 'friend' Nell Gwyn to lodge in Newport.

An important and venerable part of Newport life and one still thriving, is the Free Grammar School, which began in the year of the Armada (1588). The school was founded out of tragedy, when 'Mistress Joyce Frankland' lost her only son in a riding accident. His memorial has lasted 400 years with the present building dating from 1876. Designed by William Nesfield, this 'heart' of the present collection of buildings is of considerable architectural interest.

The daily train service that brings many of these pupils to school also provides a commuter service to London where many present day Newport residents work. Like so many other villages, its economy is no longer based on the land.

North Benfleet

The name Benfleet goes back to Saxon times. It is derived from Beam-fleote which means an inlet or creek with woods close by. North Benfleet was probably named when some of the original settlers moved further north to form a new settlement. It was also known as Little Benfleet or Benfleet Parva.

In the reign of Edward the Confessor, the manor of North Benfleet belonged to Earl Harold, later King Harold, and at the time of the Domesday survey was owned by William the Conqueror. By the 13th century it was owned by the de Benflete family, and it was probably at this time the church, All Saints, was first built. It is situated on the ridge of the hill, close by the farm of North Benfleet Hall – 'the church by the duck pond' as it is sometimes known locally. Parts of the early 13th century church remain, but much additional building and restoration took place in the 16th and 17th centuries and more in the 19th century. An interesting feature of the church is a memorial stone to John Cole, a soldier at Waterloo who was wounded by a musket ball during the famous battle and died 21 years later with the musket ball still inside him.

North Benfleet is a rural area with good farm land which has always supported several well appointed farms. North Benfleet Hall was built in late Tudor times. A priest's hole was discovered there in the 1920s and there was a substantial well built tunnel from the hall to the Sadlers Farm area which may well have been intended as an escape route for Roman Catholics during the troubled religious period of the late Tudors. There is still a farm on the site but the hall was demolished in the 1950s and all that remains is the pond which was once part of the moat. There were several moated buildings in the parish. Bradfield Farm which is now predominantly a dairy farm, has a substantial amount of its moat surviving. Some farms have changed their occupation, including Smilers Farm which is now a riding school. There are many other small business enterprises in the area, including a garden centre.

At the turn of the century parts of the large estate running from North Benfleet to Tilbury were sold off as building plots and thus the Plotlands were born. Many Londoners bought these 'little bits of land in the country' and eventually built small huts, shacks and houses on them to enable them to spend time away from the town.

Between the two World Wars, the area became more developed and more permanent buildings were erected, although it was some time before amenities such as drains, sewerage, drinking water, shops, buses etc were forthcoming. Many of these Plotland roads are still unmade and because most of them have large gardens the effect is now one of individuality and spaciousness within a still rural setting.

There is now no centre to the village as such, but many of the older buildings remain, giving a sense of history. At the corner of Pound Lane and Burnt Mills Road stands Pump Cottage which is about 400 years old, named from the nearby village pump. At the corner of Harrow Road stands Horseshoe Cottage, once the village smithy, probably about 300 years old. Also in Harrow Road was the Harrows Inn, but this closed and the local hostelry is now difficult to reach as it is across the A127, one of the busiest roads in the South East, taking commuter traffic from Southend towards London.

North Ockendon 🌿

North Ockendon is situated in the London Borough of Havering on the south eastern edge. Its name means 'oak pasture hill' but sadly there are not many oaks now.

The church dates back to pre-1075 and is approached through an avenue of lime trees. It is built of ragstone and flint with Reigate stone and has a Norman archway entrance. There are many interesting features, including a Jacobean oak pulpit, a very striking reredos of the Last Supper, thought to be Italian, and some very beautiful stained glass windows, one of which shows St Cedd (after whom the well is named).

The well is located on the left hand side of the churchyard. It derives from a natural spring which ensures a constant supply of water. It is thought that the ancient custom of judgment by 'fire and water' was held there. Legend associates the well with St Cedd who travelled around Essex using natural springs of water to baptize the local community. St Cedd was Bishop of the East Saxons (c630) and was trained at the Monastery of Lindisfarne.

The well was used in the early Middle Ages by pilgrims on their way to Canterbury as the Pilgrims Road passes close by. More recently, the well became overlooked and was very neglected. Even so, in these times of river pollution and contamination of land, it remains clean and constant even in the severest drought.

Over the past few years Mrs Joyce Cosser, a lady who used to live in the village, has taken a considerable interest in the well and, after its long years of neglect, has renovated and improved the immediate area by personally clearing back weeds, finding the original tiles which had slipped from the roof shelter, replacing them and adding her own designed heads of St Cedd and St Mary Magdalene representing the connection with the church. She has also made and tends a small garden planted around the well where flowers bloom all the year round. There is an earth and stone bank of steps leading down to the well from the churchyard.

North Weald Bassett 🌿

The earliest written references to North Weald are made in the Domesday Book in 1086. The name means 'north forest'. Bassett is from Philip de Basset, who in 1260 was the principal landowner.

St Andrew's church is the oldest building in the parish and dates from around 1330. The very fine tower was added in the early 16th century.

Wyldingtree Farm is still occupied. It was here that Simon Thorowgood was born in 1592. He became a member of the Company of Fishmongers and when he died in 1635 he left a legacy to found the original North Weald school. Wyldingtree was where the school was held during and after the Second World War, until the present school was opened in 1955.

Most people would agree that the most attractive building in the village is the Kings Head public house. The king portrayed in the sign is King Henry VIII. It is a timber framed building, which certainly looks Tudor. It is not certain how old the present building is, but parts may date from the 16th century.

The airfield was used in the First World War, but it became well known as a fighter base in the Battle of Britain. Several famous people were stationed there, including Sir Douglas Bader, the legless pilot, and Sir Thomas Pike, who was Marshal of the RAF. Pike Way, which was a former officers quarters, is named after him. In 1952 Princess Astrid of Norway unveiled a memorial on the airfield in memory of the many Norwegians who flew from the station. A large estate, built on the old airfield in 1984, has all the roads named after aircraft.

At the entrance to Harrison Drive, in the centre of the village, stands the village sign, a Hurricane aircraft with a hangar in the background. This is taken from a painting by a local artist, Valerie Rush. The Hurricane shown was an aircraft used on the airfield. This sign was placed there by money raised in the village during the Queen's Silver Jubilee.

Harrison Drive is named in memory of the Harrison family,

who previously lived on the site in Yew Tree Cottage. Miss Violet and Miss Maud Harrison were well known, not just locally. Violet was president of the British Goat Society, and bred a world champion goat, which appeared on pre-war television at Alexandra Palace. When Mahatma Gandhi stayed in this country, it was from the Weald herd that he was supplied with goats milk.

Since 1921 the skyline at North Weald has been dominated by radio masts belonging to the radio station. The largest of these masts were removed in 1982. There are still many small ones left, although the station itself was closed in October 1985. On the radio station site is an old fort which was built in 1889. Although known as Ongar Radio Station, the majority of the site is in the parish of Stanford Rivers.

Old Harlow 🦡

Harlow now has a population of more than 70,000 and is one of the original five new towns built soon after the Second World War to house the overspill from London. However the old village from which it derives its name stands proudly on its north-eastern boundary and retains much of its original charm and character.

It has a long history dating back at least to Roman times. Its name comes from the Saxon 'here' or host, and 'hlaw' a hill, indicating the moot held near to a mound or hill. A tumulus still survives near Mulberry Green House.

A Roman temple has been excavated near the river Stort, and a Norman chapel (Harlowbury) was for many years used as a granary. Now it has been restored, and evidence of an earlier Saxon building has been found.

There has been a church located in Churchgate Street since early times, but it was destroyed by fire in 1708, after which the local gentry vied with each other in the restoration work and many embellishments were added. Between 1878 and 1880 the church was almost entirely pulled down, and rebuilt with much taste and care. The old brasses and monuments have been carefully re-sited and date from the early 15th century.

Harlow is very rich in charities and endowments, some of them of a very interesting nature. Newman, Stafford and Reeve all endowed almshouses. George Benson left a cottage and land, the income from which was to provide coats and breeches of drab cloth for poor men, and linsey-woolsey petticoats for poor women, all of them to be marked with his initials GB. John Wright, executor for the Staffords, left £150 to provide an annual sermon and dinner for the Stafford trustees, and clothing and fuel for the widows in the Stafford almshouses.

One of Harlow's claims to fame came in the reign of Queen Elizabeth I when her court visited Mark Hall mansion. This estate lies to the west of the village, and though the big house was burnt down in 1947, mercifully the lovely church (St Mary at Latton) remains and is well worth a visit. It contains, among many notable memorials, one to James Altham and his wife Dame Mary Judd who entertained Queen Elizabeth I on three separate occasions.

Although Mark Hall was destroyed, much of the magnificent parkland which surrounded it still survives as open space in the new town, and the stable block has been transformed into a splendid Cycle Museum. This houses a unique collection of bicycles and memorabilia acquired from Mr John Collins whose family had a bicycle shop in Market Street for many years.

Many of the old buildings are of architectural and historic interest, especially those situated in Churchgate Street, Mulberry Green and Market Street. An old coaching inn, now the Green Man hotel, reputedly has a permanent ghostly resident.

Paglesham 🚲

While only a few miles from Southend, Paglesham still has a feeling of being remote. The tidal waters which surround it on north, east and south have protected it from development, so that visitors find a peace and space remarkable to the town dweller.

The tide has influenced the development of the village from earliest times. 'Redhills' indicate salt manufacture back to Roman times. A Saxon, Paccel, may have started the village. Certainly there was a church before 1066, the living was given to Westminster Abbey in that year. Norman windows remain. Sheep grazing the flat marshlands probably paid for the handsome 15th century tower which ends the road at Church End. Waterside Lane appropriately takes the other half of Paglesham – East End back to the sea wall and Shuttlewood's Boat Yard.

Oysters, boats and smuggling provided excitement in the past. Hard-Apple Blyth combined all three at the end of the 18th century. In quieter times, William Blyth became the village grocer and churchwarden. He is reputed to have used the church records to wrap up the butter. Certainly, the parish records do not go back much before his time. He died in 1830 aged 74. His tombstone can be seen in the churchyard on the north side of the chancel.

Cupola House is a handsome Georgian farmhouse built in 1803 which was reputedly paid for by money made out of smuggling. From the cupola, long gone, although the stairs remain, it was possible to watch the Excise men on the sea wall. Goods were hidden in a variety of places, including hollow garden walls at Cupola House.

James Wiseman was a member of one of the Wiseman families, engaged in the hard, but lucrative oyster business. He expanded the Chase to its large Victorian form, installing fountains and greenhouses in the garden and building the stables, farm buildings and cottages which form much of East End today.

Today, Paglesham is much more tranquil than in the past. Wheat, rape and peas cover most of the farmland, but few of the villagers are needed to bring them to harvest. Sheep still graze, but the oyster industry is minimal. However, an Annual Festival (Oyster) stimulates the local pubs to culinary heights and the waterside is alive in summer with recreational boats of all sizes.

Rayleigh ✼

Rayleigh was once a small village of approximately 5000 inhabitants, mostly farmers and land workers. It had a wide tree-lined High Street with lovely old houses and bow fronted shops and cottages, and plenty of coaching inns – five of which are still plying their trade. One 400 year old shop in the High Street has a long loft the entire length of the house and garden and was Rayleigh's first dance hall, the platform where the fiddlers played still stands.

Rayleigh was very much an educational centre having several old established schools. Henson's school took in boarders from all over Essex. The parish room was a church school for 6d a week, and the Baptist chapel also had a school in its grounds. Another old house near the church was a finishing school for young ladies in 1895.

The first telephone exchange was housed in Patmore's baker's shop. When the bread had to be taken from the oven Mrs Patmore had to leave the exchange board and the clerks in the nearby offices would have to run across to put their calls through, causing some delay!

The Mount was an 11th century motte and bailey castle and Henry VIII often hunted in its grounds.

Sir Bernard Braine who resides in Rayleigh was the local M.P. for 35 years and is now Father of the House. He was recently made a Knight of the Papal Order of the Holy Sepulchre, an honour seldom given to those outside of Holy Orders and also given the Greek Order of Honour.

Rayleigh was famous for its carnival from about 1900 until 1957. A horse fair had been held in Rayleigh from time immemorial in the High Street, and the last one was held in 1919 to celebrate the peace.

Rayne ✺

Rayne is an ancient village situated on the A120, two miles from Braintree and nine from Dunmow. The A120 is Stane Street, where Roman soldiers progressed along the route made to link Colchester and St Albans. Now container traffic speeds through from Felixstowe and Harwich to the M11.

Rayne is in the heart of Essex farmland, sprinkled with attractive Tudor farmhouses, and in the Street itself are fine examples of clothier's houses of a slightly later period.

The population has increased to over 3,000 in the past 20 years as modern housing developments have brought young families and a commuter coach link with London.

The Rayne and Braintree bypass is presently under construction, and the new dual carriageway A120 is in its final planning stage. These roads will restore a more peaceful atmosphere to the village. The full impact of Stansted airport is still to be felt, although further housing development relating to the airport has been rejected.

Miss Eliza Vaughan was a celebrated local authoress of books dealing with Essex village life. She lived for over 50 years at

Turners in Stane Street. In one of her articles she recounted the history of her house. In 1616 it was sold to Simon and Ann Bridge of Felsted. Their son John set sail for America in the *Lyon* in 1632, and was the founder of a school in New Town, three miles west of Boston. This became the first University College in America and should have been named after Bridge, but John Harvard who went out later, died soon afterwards leaving all his money and half his library to the establishment. He was a young Cambridge professor, and so the town was re-named Cambridge and the college called by his name, although Bridge was its Principal, and his statue stands before the entrance to Harvard.

Hopefully Rayne will retain its peaceful rural characteristics well into the future. It has its farms, Rayne Foundry and other small industrial undertakings, its church, school, splendid village hall and especially its societies. The latest of these are the Rayne Village Society and the Rayne Help Scheme which care in turn for the environment of Rayne and its inhabitants.

Rochford ❧

Just over three miles north of Southend, Rochford is steeped in history. It was mentioned in the Domesday Book and the first village settlement was by the Romans in the 2nd century.

Along South Street you will come to the cruciform where the four roads converge as on the compass – North Street, South Street, East Street and West Street. This cruciform is one of the few remaining in this country. South Street itself can boast many old and well maintained properties dating back many years.

Weir Pond Road, aptly named many years ago, still has many of the old original cottages, now listed buildings and revelling in such delightful names as Lilac Cottage, Rose Cottage, etc. You can turn right into East Street, again passing many fine old houses. On the right is King's Hill, once known as the 'Lawless Court', and the home of the Whispering Post, one of the well known features of Rochford.

The hub of Rochford is the Market Square. Originally it housed many old wooden buildings and every Thursday a cattle market was held. This was a feature for miles around and continued until 1959.

There were two fires here – one being accidental but causing a great deal of damage. The second was on the occasion of the Relief of Mafeking when a bonfire was again lit, causing much damage. According to records there was also an execution in the Square. The victim was a religious martyr by the name of Henry Simson. A plaque still exists to commemorate this and can be seen in one of the alleyways leading off the square.

Down West Street, past the station, on the right are the alms-houses, built by Lord Rich, and still occupied. The lovely old parish church of St Andrews stands in the middle of the Rochford Golf Course. It is said to be the only church standing in a golf course. This truly is a beautiful church, kept in immaculate condition.

Standing opposite the Church is Rochford Hall, with its twisted chimneys and one of Rochford's most historic buildings. It was originally the home of the Boleyn family where King Henry VIII held many trysts with Anne Boleyn.

Rowhedge 🌿

Rowhedge has a population of 2,000 and is part of the parish of East Donyland. It is only three miles from Colchester but by keeping the Green Belt intact it is still an independent village. The river Colne is on the eastern side, Roman river on the south side, (the Roman river nature walk starts from the river Colne and follows the Roman river to Oliver's Orchard Centre at Stanway), the army firing range on the west includes Donyland Woods, with footpaths through to Mersea Road, and the green belt of farmland is on the north.

During the Second World War gravel was extracted from farm-land between the village and Roman river, which was loaded onto boats from a small quay and used, it is said, for building aero-dromes. Ninety acres of land were left derelict but during the last 15 years the quay has been expanded into a wharf and 30 acres have been covered with warehousing.

Rowhedge really flourished in Victorian times, when the men caught herrings and sprats in the winter and manned the big yachts in the summer. There were two shipyards, one building 200 ton brigs and barques and the other building smacks and yachts.

The brewery, which was in production at the turn of the century, known as Donyland Brewery and later Daniels Brewery, loaded the beer onto barges which conveyed it round the coast, sometimes up to London. There was a clothing factory from about 1910 until very recently, making quality alpaca coats, jackets and during the war Army Officer's uniforms.

The little hexagonal church of St Lawrence was built in 1838. There is also a small Methodist church and a Mariners' Chapel first built for the seamen and taken over by the Datchet Trust in recent years. The villagers have built their own community centre and the British Legion has its own hall and provides social activities. There are still three public houses, who provide meals. The Anchor is very popular with the room overlooking the river. The elderly are catered for with several flats, and the Paget Memorial Cottages were specially built for aged yacht hands. There is also an old people's home which in earlier days was the Coronation Bakery.

Runwell ✤

Situated on low hills near the river Crouch to the north and east of Wickford, Runwell is approximately 12 miles from Chelmsford and a similar distance from Southend-on-Sea.

At its south-western end, close to the Wickford boundary, lies the parish church of St Mary. Its grey, stone tower dates back to the 15th century but the round columns of the arcades are from a church which was a place of pilgrimage in the 12th century, Thomas Becket's time. Decoration of the timber of the porches bears Tudor roses and on one of its doors, now curtained, is a strange burnt mark which legend says is the mark of the devil's hand when one summer's day he was shut in the church by a corrupt priest, Rainaldus, who dabbled in the 'black arts'.

Rainaldus, it is said, vanished in a bubbling, hissing pool of evil-smelling black liquid, which sank beneath the brick floor of the south porch, leaving a circular stain wherein could be seen a strange skull-like flint. Doubtless on account of its superstitious connection this was subsequently thrown away, but in 1944 a stone was discovered in the churchyard shaped as the legend described. Until recently it was set into the south wall of the church surrounded by an inscription in Latin, the translation being 'The wages of sin is death'. This flint is now housed in Southend's central museum.

Monuments to members of the Sulyard family grace the walls of the chancel including brasses of Eustace Sulyard and his wife in ruffs facing each other across a prayer desk. The Sulyards lived in what is now Flemings Farm, the present building consisting of the remnants of the north-east wing of a once extensive Tudor mansion. Sited in the north of the parish, it is close to Poplars Farm, due east of which is the Running Well from which Runwell received its name. The spring which feeds the well has never been known to fail and the well can be found at the highest point in the parish where three fields meet.

Despite the village's proximity to Wickford and an enormous increase in population from 350 inhabitants in 1924 to just under 5,000 at the present time, it has a strong community spirit and links with Chelmsford, the county town, are cherished.

St Osyth ✺

St Osyth, situated between Colchester and Clacton, was originally called Chich, which means creek. The official name of the parish is Chich St Osyth, although the 'Chich' is not used.

Osyth, daughter of the first Christian king of the East Angles founded a nunnery in Chich. In the 7th century a Danish pirate fleet is said to have landed along the coast of the creek burning and looting the countryside. When Osyth refused to worship their pagan gods they chopped off her head; where she fell a spring of fresh water spouted from the ground. This spring is in Nuns Wood on the Priors estate. This part of the estate is not open to the public.

The creek was, up until the outbreak of the First World War, widely used by barges. They would arrive laden with coal or timber and stay for several days. A number of these barges helped in the evacuation of Dunkirk, and sadly some did not come back. There is now a boatyard by the creek and barges once more have returned, this time not laden but to be repaired.

In 1413 a tidal mill was built at St Osyth creek. This was used for grinding corn. Before the Second World War it was commonplace to see artists sketching the mill. Unfortunately it was damaged during the war and finally collapsed in 1961–62.

Perhaps St Osyth is best known for the Priory. The gatehouse completed in 1475 is considered to be one of the finest monastic buildings in the country. Throughout the 18th and the first half of the 19th centuries the Priory estate was owned by the Earls of Rochford. Since 1857, when the last of the Rochfords died the Priors has had a number of owners.

The St Osyth witch trials in 1582 have been described as the most infamous of all English witch trials. Six women were sentenced to death, one of these being Ursula Kemp. The village 'lock up' was situated in Colchester Road next to the Kings Arms. It was alleged that Ursula Kemp was imprisoned there until her trial.

In 1921 a skeleton was found in a garden in Mill Street. The skeleton was bound and nailed and it was thought to be that of one of the executed witches. Coach loads of tourists would arrive in the summer to view the skeleton. In 1932 the house in whose garden the skeleton lay was burnt to the ground. Some people thought it was because the witch had been disturbed, so her grave once more was filled in. In the 1950s the skeleton was taken to a museum at Boscastle in Cornwall.

The village has changed completely. Very few people work on farms and most people commute to work in London or other towns. The farm cottages are now desirable country houses. Many estates have been built and very few people living in the village are village born and bred.

The Sampfords 🌿

The village of Great Sampford, and the larger parish of Little Sampford are the archetypal example of English country life. Although many people work outside the village, even commute to London, farming is still the lifeblood and mainstay of the community.

The origins of the Sampfords, meaning sandy ford, are still awaiting discovery but it is known there was a Saxon settlement about the river Pant, where the kingfisher is often seen. Mentioned in Domesday the names were Sanfort (Magna) and Sanforda

(Parva), when the population numbered between 275 to 325. Nine hundred years later there are around 650 residents.

Dovehouse Farm at Tindon End was the scene in 1896 of the discovery of a 4,000 year old stone axe head, now exhibited at Saffron Walden Museum. A bronze snake bracelet dates from Roman times and was also found in the Sampford area. This is now in the Cambridge University Museum.

The two churches are still in use. St Michael the Archangel at Great Sampford dates from the 13th century. St Michael's setting is idyllic, at the heart of the village, above the river Pant, surrounded by a flint stone wall and bordered by an avenue of lime trees. The view to the west is across miles of undulating Essex cornland and woodland.

St Mary the Virgin at Little Sampford is enchanting. Set in a fold of the land its churchyard must be one of the most picturesque. Local artists often sketch there and villagers and visitors alike seem to savour its special peacefulness with the view across the river valley. The present building is believed to date from early in the 1300s, although there has been a church on the site since well before the Norman Conquest. Great efforts were made by parishioners to raise the thousands of pounds needed to restore the beautiful east window.

The Sampfords have a school, a Victorian village hall, a post office, two garages and two pubs, The Bull and The Red Lion. There is also a flourishing tennis club, as well as a cricket team and drama group.

Some of the old farms have names dating from the original owners in medieval times. The oldest, Free Roberts, is named after Walter FitzRobert, who annually paid 1d or a pair of white gloves for land at Great Sampford. The oldest name in Little Sampford dates from 1280; Hawkes Farm, on the lane to Cornish Hall End. The beautiful Tewes is named after Richard Tewes and dates from 1483. It is in a secret valley just below the woodland known as High Trees which leads to Little Sampford church.

Clock House was known as Home Farm until the clock was made by John Pettit in 1778. The Brook family have occupied it for over 75 years. Another Pettit, Richard, founded the Baptist chapel. His sons were millers. Pettit Hill has now become Mill Hill. Later Richard's grandson, John, moved to the famous Grantchester Mill immortalized by Rupert Brooke.

Sandon 🌿

Sandon is a small village, to the south-east of Chelmsford, with a Norman church dedicated to St Andrew.

Runaway brides in the 17th century did not all have to dash to far away Scotland in order to obtain a quick wedding as the rector of Sandon, the Reverend Gilbert Dillingham, was only too ready to oblige.

As news of his willingness and cooperation spread through and beyond the county, weddings at Sandon, which had averaged four per year, increased enormously. Between 1615 and 1635 the Reverend Dillingham married no fewer than 511 couples, including a daughter of the rector of Chelmsford, using an assumed surname as apparently did lots of others. The parson undoubtedly grew fat on the wedding fees.

His successor, the Rev Brian Walton, who later became chaplain to King Charles II and was eventually made Bishop of Chester, put an immediate stop to these irregularities, to the intense disappointment and grief of those runaways who still turned up expecting to obtain the services of Mr Dillingham!

Sewards End 🌿

Sewards End lies two miles east of the market town of Saffron Walden. It sits on the edge of a clay plateau, 150 feet above the Walden valley, and is reached by a winding road, which was once a river bed. Sprinkled along a mile of main road (B1053), there are 143 dwellings, housing around 350 inhabitants. Besides the houses, there is a shop, public house, a small church, village hall, a garage and several large outlying farms.

Over the past 50 years, Sewards End has changed from a mainly agricultural society to one which includes a high percentage of business and professional people, many of whom commute to London.

At the time of the Norman Conquest, there was nothing here but a tangle of ancient, marshy forest. Sewards End began when Geoffrey de Mandeville, Lord of Saffron Walden, granted 60 acres of land to Sigisweard (pronounced Sayward) the Dane, who was, reputedly, his food taster. When Sigisweard died, in 1114, the land passed to his grandson, Albold de Pouncyn. Pounce Hall still stands on the village boundary, and, although not the original building, part of it dates back to 1460.

During the 13th century several more land grants were made, the largest to John de Maten, and the twin hamlets of Sewards End and Mattens developed side by side until the 15th century when the Black Death caused the collapse of both estates. The land was acquired by the powerful Saffron Walden monastery, and amalgamated under the single name of Sewards End.

Following the dissolution of the monasteries, in the 16th century, it became part of the Audley estates, a situation which remained, basically, unchanged until the present century.

One house, which now belies its age, is Everards. Believed to be a 14th century yeoman's farm, it was originally built round a communal hall, with a central fireplace. One eye-catching feature is the thatched coach house. Possibly older, is Campions, noted for its unique wall paintings, discovered some years ago, and now in Saffron Walden museum. And, nearby, stands the water tower, built in 1905. For 65 years, water was pumped into the tower, twice a day, from the artesian wells in Saffron Walden.

The Towers was built between 1830–50 by an eccentric, William Gayton. It is a folly, intended as a mini-version of the famous Audley End palace. Besides being eccentric, William was also belligerent, and spent 20 years fighting, often literally, with successive builders. He managed to complete his grandiose scheme, but was declared bankrupt in 1851 and died a year later in the workhouse. For a time, the house was occupied by his brother, Thomas, before becoming The Towers College, a public school. Since 1875, it has been a private residence.

Another memorial to the Gayton family is the village church, built by Thomas Gayton in 1847. He later added a school room, which was used, not only by village children, but also those from Saffron Walden workhouse.

Sewardstone 🌿

Sewardstone lies on the river Lee between Chingford and Waltham Abbey. It sits astride the Greenwich Meridian and part of it comes within the area of the Lee Valley Regional Park.

The manor of Sewardstone comprises the hamlets of Sewardstone, Sewardstonebury and that part of Epping Forest that is called High Beach – the 'Cockney's Paradise'. The earliest houses date from about 1600 with all styles and periods being represented. Notable buildings include the parish church, a primary school that caters for about 70 children, two village halls, a conservation centre run by the Field Studies Council, a youth hostel and seven pubs! Villagers lost their shop recently, but its place has to an extent been taken by a nearby farm shop.

Sewardstone has worldwide connections through Gilwell Park, which has been a training centre for the Scout and Guide Associations since 1919. The park itself is much older than that, and one of the buildings, the White House, is supposed to be haunted.

Many interesting people have lived in the area. The most famous was Alfred, Lord Tennyson, who wrote part of *In Memoriam* here. The 'wild bells' referred to are said to be the bells of Waltham Abbey. An earlier poet, John Clare, was a patient at Dr Matthew Allen's progressive lunatic asylum, which was spread over three large houses at Lippitts Hill.

The infamous Dick Turpin is supposed to have lived at Sewardstonebury. Certainly he had several hideouts in the area and did some of his most dreadful deeds here, too! His ghost is said to ride down a nearby hill with an old woman clinging to his back. The story is that he once tortured an old woman by sitting her on her own fire to make her tell where her valuables were.

Sadly, no traditional customs or pastimes have survived, but villagers do have the right to graze cattle in the forest and to gather fallen wood – no longer than a man's arm and no thicker than his wrist.

During the Second World War there was a POW camp here. Many of the prisoners were Italians and when the war ended some of them stayed here to establish themselves in the local glasshouse industry. This still provides employment for a number of local people. Other local sources of employment are numerous riding stables and boarding kennels, several farms and, of course, the pubs! Other residents follow a wide variety of trades and professions.

For several hundreds of years, the Royal Gunpowder Works has been established in the area. Indeed, the gunpowder which was used in the Gunpowder Plot was probably made here. The famous Enfield rifles certainly were. Both these works are gradually being closed down, and the thump of the underground test explosions will become a thing of the past.

Shalford

Whenever visitors come to Shalford they invariably comment on the beauty of the area. Lying as it does in the valley of the river Pant, Shalford is one of a string of pretty North Essex villages stretching towards the Cambridgeshire border.

It is surrounded by farmland which, in most cases, has belonged to the same families for generations and must seem rather sleepy, possessing only one general store cum post office, a school and two pubs.

However, the appearance of inactivity is deceptive as there are many clubs and organisations catering for every age group and making life busy for the local inhabitants. From the first rummage sale in the spring, through the shows, fetes and barbecues of the summer to the Christmas carol concert.

The church is small, simple and beautiful, the oldest building in the village which has a mixture of architectural styles from the 16th century to the new. Most newcomers quickly take their places in the community, their children attend the village school and become welcome new villagers in the changing countryside.

Sible Hedingham

Sible Hedingham, mentioned in the Domesday Book, is now a flourishing and expanding village and the centre for secondary education in the rural north-eastern corner of Essex. Although there has been much new building the earlier village is still evident in the cluster of old cottages around the 14th century church of St Peter, and in the areas of the three streams that feed into the river Colne.

Industry developed along the now disused railway line and together with farming played an important part in the prosperity of the district. The numerous brickworks have long disappeared but the joinery firm is still the major employer.

The Colne Valley Railway, Sible Hedingham

A famous son of the village is Sir John Hawkwood who was born in Hawkwood Manor about 1320. He fought in the French Wars under both the Black Prince and Edward III at the battles of Crecy and Poitiers and received the honour of a knighthood for his outstanding services.

After the wars he formed a company of mercenaries which became known as the White Company, carrying white pennants and wearing white surcoats. They fought for whoever hired them amongst the various Italian independent states. Sir John and his White Company were both respected and feared and the troop settled down as the unofficial army of the Florentine Republic. In March of 1394 as an old man of over 70 his 'heart grew sick for home' and he was preparing to return to England and take up his inheritance of Hawkwood Manor, on the death of his elder brother, when he died suddenly.

The Florentines, who held him in high esteem, gave him a

143

magnificent state funeral. A monument was erected to his memory in Florence Cathedral where it can still be seen. The inscription on this called him 'John Hawkwood a British Knight the most cautious leader of his age'.

After his father's death young John Hawkwood returned to England and the manor of Hawkwood. He is considered to have rebuilt the village church of St Peter and there are carved stone hawks on the tower and in other parts of the church. There is a picture of the Florentine Memorial in the church.

Springfield 🌿

Archaeologists are still investigating the site where Iron Age man made the first settlement of the area some 5000 years ago. Almost 2000 years ago the invading Roman armies passed by the site, and during their occupation of the country built the first road direct from London to Colchester. Springfield Road is still on that direct line.

A mere 900 years ago the Domesday Book recorded that, among other things, Springfield had two flourishing fish ponds which helped to feed the residents. One of those ponds still exists close to the boundary of the parish.

Among the Norman invaders who came with William, Sir Walter Tyrell, who was given many estates in the area, is still commemorated in the name given to Tyrells Close. In the early 15th century one of his descendants became the first Baronet of Springfield, and although that title did not survive for more than five generations people with the name of Tyrell still live in the area.

Norman builders laid the foundations of the village church, and although it has been extensively restored and added to, it is still possible to see traces of the original work.

During the religious bigotry of the early 17th century a Springfield churchwarden, William Pinchion emigrated to America and founded a settlement which has grown into the great city of Springfield, Massachusetts. During the Second World War, many US servicemen operating from airfields in Essex took the opportunity of visiting the original Springfield, and even now parties of tourists still come over to visit the village of their founder.

Shortly after the execution of King Charles I Springfield was visited by one of Oliver Cromwell's sequestrators who recorded that in the church chancel was a brass memorial to 'Thomas de Coggeshall Esq, who died on 18th February 1421'. From other sources it is known that he was one of the knights who had accompanied Henry V to the battle of Agincourt where they defeated the French. Unfortunately the brass has become very badly worn, and its lettering obliterated. Only when the sequestrator's records came to light early in the 20th century was it possible to establish the true record.

Stambridge ✣

In the Domesday Book mention is made of the manors of Little Stambridge (Stanbruge) and Great Stambridge (Stanbruge), actually meaning Stonebridge. It is thought that at this time there were four small settlements in the area, with a total of approximately 17 families plus one slave family.

Present day Stambridge is a very small village situated about 7 miles from Southend-on-Sea. There is the modernised Royal Oak public house and village store and post office, surrounded by a collection of cottages and bungalows opposite which there is the Baptist chapel. A long narrow strip of land bounds the river Roach. Along the main road in a south westerly direction is the Memorial Hall and on the opposite side of the road stands the old rectory, now a nursing home, as well as the present day rectory. Further along in the same direction is the Stambridge church of St Mary and All Saints. Parts of the original Saxon building can be seen, but it is difficult to say exactly how long a church has stood on this site.

The most famous inhabitant of Stambridge is John Winthrop, 1588–1649. In 1630 he and his family set sail for America in the *Arbella*. Not only was John Winthrop the first Governor of Boston, having been elected in London the previous year as Governor of The Massachusetts Bay Company, he also helped to found the American shipbuilding industry which has made the port of Boston famous throughout the world. John Winthrop died on 26th March 1649, his grave is in the burial ground next to Kings Chapel, Boston, the oldest Anglican church in New England which later, in 1785 became the first Unitarian church in America.

Considerable interest in Stambridge is still maintained by the Winthrop family in America who, in 1970 paid for the making and installation of a stained glass memorial window depicting the *Arbella*. Americans visiting this country will often travel to Stambridge to view the 'Winthrop Window'. In 1983 there were 2 signatures in the visitors book who described themselves as 12th and 13th descendants of the first John Winthrop.

Stanford Rivers 🍂

Stanford goes back to Anglo Saxon times as 'stan' meant stoney, a ford across the river Roding. Rivers was added in King John's time through the Rivers family. St Margaret's church is still under royal patronage.

Although a considerable number of houses have been built since the First World War, Stanford Rivers remains a rural place. Unfortunately many of its lovely trees and hedges have been lost but the scattered farms and cottages still have their place in its history and character. There are two separate hamlets, namely Toot Hill and Little End, a few miles apart. The latter stretches along the London Road and has old and new houses. The old Union House (workhouse) is now Piggotts Tent factory, known world wide and which provides the huge tent at the Chelsea Flower Show. Dating back to the 11th century is Littlebury Water Mill in the process of being restored.

Opposite the factory is the site of the Congregational church, where a few headstones of graves still remain – the chapel was burnt down in 1927. It was here that David Livingstone, the famous missionary and explorer was to have preached his first sermon. One Sunday evening he was sent to take the service at the chapel by the Rev Richard Cecil, who trained students at the Ongar church. All went well until after giving out his text his mind went blank and he apologised and left the chapel in great distress. However, he was given another chance and later became a renowned figure.

There are four public houses in the parish. Two on the London road no doubt were 'stops' for the daily stage coaches to and from London. They are the White Bear and the Woodman. Toot Hill also has a very popular inn, the Green Man, and between Ongar and Toot Hill on the borders of Greensted and Stanford Rivers is the Drill House. Here you will see a red Victorian letter box let into the house wall with the name Repentance on its times of collection notice!

The 'Chrisom Memorial' is in St Margaret's church. Near the altar is the little flat stone with a brass covering. It is of a child wrapped in his chrisom robe. It is in memory of Thomas Greville (1442), son of Giles Greville. This denotes that the baby died within a month of his baptism and was buried in swaddling clothes. This is believed to be one of only two such memorials existing today.

Church of St Margaret, Stanford Rivers

Stansted Mountfitchet

Stansted Mountfitchet is a very old village mentioned in the Domesday Book as Stansteda. Its name is derived from this and from Richard de Montfitchet who lived in the castle of which only a very small piece of walling remains. This knight was reputed to be the youngest and one of the three bravest in England. He is immortalised on the village signs at each end of the village which show the Norman knight in full splendour.

A re-constructed Norman wooden motte and bailey castle has been built on the site of the original castle and has fast become a popular tourist spot.

A stroll around the lanes, footpaths and roads shows many types of buildings from all periods. There are two lovely churches in complete contrast, one dating from the 12th century and the other a fine example of Victorian architecture.

Enter Stansted Mountfitchet from the south and over the crest of the hill by the Old Bell public house, you will see before you the magnificent sight of the Stansted windmill, especially striking on a dark evening when floodlit.

It was built in 1787, together with a villa, malthouse and bakehouse. The wooden malthouse with its thatched roof caught fire and was burnt down in 1877 and the bakehouse too has disappeared, but the miller's villa still stands and is now used as a Roman Catholic church.

The mill has passed through many hands and had many alterations in its 200 years. James Blyth, who was later the first Baron Blyth of Stansted Mountfitchet, acquired the mill in 1887. The 2nd Lord Blyth had extensive repairs done in 1930 and in 1935 conveyed the mill 'for the benefit of the inhabitants of Stansted', with the Parish Council and Mr Rex Wailes as co-trustees. From 1941 until 1963 it was used as the Scout headquarters.

In 1952 the windmill was declared an Ancient Monument and a great deal of restoration work has since taken place.

Stanway 🦚

Stanway is situated three miles west of Colchester and has, as part of its boundary from the town, Grymes Dyke, now the only Iron Age dyke in the United Kingdom. It is a large village covering some four square miles and at one time known as Great Stanway and Little Stanway, forming part of the great forest of Essex.

Stanway, or 'Stoneway', took its name from the old Roman road, Stane Street, running from Bishops Stortford to Colchester through the centre of the village, which is now London Road. At the eastern end of the road is situated the old Union Workhouse erected to house 200 paupers, where many a vagrant could be seen making his way for a night's lodging: it is now a home for the elderly. At the western end, on Swan Green, the annual sheep fairs used to be held and an oak tree was planted there to commemorate the Coronation of Edward VII. Nearby, at the farm, was the parish pound, now stabling.

Stane Street was used by many a pilgrim on his way to Walsingham. On the site of the now parish church, St Albright's, stood a small Saxon chapel, which it is thought could have been an oratory chapel and, therefore, a place of pilgrimage itself with Albright, a holy man and hermit, living in a crude hut dwelling next door. The weary travellers could refresh themselves at three nearby inns; the Swan, still a flourishing eating house, the White Hart, now a nursery and once the rose gardens of Cant's Roses, and The Turkeycock, now converted into houses. The poor folk would camp in the fields opposite the little chapel where Miracle and Mystery plays were performed and stalls set up giving the area the name of 'Playing Stalls'. Almshouses are now on this site.

Gradually, from the 14th century, St Albright's church was built and extended. During 1826 a Queen Anne card table served for an altar beneath which the parish library was kept, the rector's butler dispensing books on Sunday after divine service!

The original parish church, All Saints, was situated by another Roman road in the south of the village about two miles away. It gradually fell into disrepair and it is reputed that half of it was torn down by Parliamentary men to help with materials for the Great Siege of Colchester. Today it has far more attention, for Stanway Hall, in whose grounds it is situated, is now a zoo and the church ruins provide a background to owls and birds of prey.

The Domesday Book quotes Stanway as possessing three mills so it must have been a prosperous agricultural area. Much of this land is now gouged out into deep pits, for underneath the crop growing soil was discovered an abundance of sand and gravel; for many years the residents have become attuned to the familiar sight and sound of the continual flow of lorries.

Steeple Bumpstead ✑

Nurse Edith Cavell died in Brussels on 12th October 1915, shot by a German firing squad for helping Allied soldiers to escape. She became, of course, a legend for bravery and sacrifice. But her ties with Steeple Bumpstead occurred long before that and before she became a nurse. During 1886, Edith was appointed governess to the four children of the Reverend Charles Powell, vicar of Steeple Bumpstead.

The vicarage is no longer the residence of the local vicar, but it is still there, a private residence, on the corner of Chapel Street and Finchingfield Road. There is, in the 11th century village church, a plaque dedicated to Edith Cavell and there is also a road named after her.

There has been a long history of non-conformist belief in the village. A Bumpstead man was burnt to death in the parish for his beliefs in the days of the Catholic church. Along the Blois Road, leading from Bumpstead to Birdbrook, is a field that has been called the 'Bloody Pightle', and that is where he is believed to have been martyred.

Later John Tibauld and eight other village residents were seized and taken before the Bishop of London, charged with meeting together in Bower Hall to pray and read a copy of the New Testament. Although the non-conformists in the village were encouraged by the powerful Bendyshe family that lived at Bower Hall, even their influence could not save Tibauld. He was burned at the stake.

One haunting that is rumoured in Steeple Bumpstead centres on the old mansion of Bower Hall. It is said that the children's nurse dropped or threw her employer's baby from the nursery window. Her ghost is said to walk the area of the Camping Close near to where the house originally stood. But the building, if that is what she seeks, is no longer there. It was removed and rebuilt, brick by brick, in America!

Stifford 🦋

Anyone going along High Road, North Stifford, must be intrigued by the thatched cottages, St Mary's church, and the very pleasant village green. North Stifford is the old part of the parish of Stifford which nowadays is identified by three areas – North Stifford, South Stifford and Stifford Clays.

For over 800 years Stifford was a small village with houses along the High Road, the church at the east end and the public house at the west end. Stage coaches on their way from Southend to London called at the Dog and Partridge (the village inn) as a staging post.

From the 16th to the 20th century there were three large houses – Stifford Hall later replaced by Stifford Lodge, Coppid Hall, and Ford Place. The two principal farms were Chalk Pit Farm and Stifford Clays Farm on the south and east borders.

In this century housing and road development have radically changed the character of the village. In 1926 the A13 (now A1013) and in the early 1980s a new trunk road (the present A13) have split the village of North Stifford and divided it from Stifford Clays and South Stifford. Of the large houses Stifford Lodge is a Moat House hotel, Coppid Hall has been converted into flats, and of Ford Place only a shell remains. It was destroyed by arson in 1986. Stifford Clays farm was largely swallowed up by housing in the post Second World War period. Chalk Pit farm is isolated from the village and is due to be developed for building.

In 1980 an interesting find linked the 14th and 20th centuries. Pilgrims on their way to Canterbury used to cross the Thames at South Stifford and would have passed over Stifford Bridge. One of them lost one of his pilgrim's seals near the bridge. The seals were worn in the pilgrims' hats – they seem to have been the 14th century equivalent of 'car stickers'. The pilgrim who lost his seal by Stifford Bridge was obviously on a grand tour. The seal depicts St Peter holding the keys of the Kingdom, and St Paul holding a sword. This seal would have originated in Rome. It was placed in Thurrock's local history museum.

Richard Baker Wingfield was lord of the manor of Orsett and Stifford from 1859–80. He was a good landlord and local benefactor. Many of the farm improvements can still be seen, as, for instance, the stockyard and large barn at Chalkpit Farm. He provided and endowed the parochial school in the High Road in 1840, well before the advent of compulsory education in 1871.

On the death of Mr Wingfield Baker, Stifford, with the Orsett estate, passed to the Whitmore family, and remained under their control until the death of Sir Francis Whitmore in 1962. This marked the start of the development of present day Stifford. The estate and houses were bought by many private individuals. Some of the farmland on the south bank of the Mardyke river was bought by the Thurrock Council and is now a Country Park.

Stock ✑

The full name is really Stock Harvard, but 'Harvard' is little used today except for ecclesiastical purposes.

The village is on a hill, not quite so high as Danbury or Langdon Hills, but high enough to give delightful views in almost every direction over the surrounding typical Essex undulating countryside.

The name goes back to Saxon times, and the Saxon word for 'wood' was 'stok', indicating that at one time, the countryside around here was a part of the great forest which covered much of this portion of Essex. 'Harvard' is a derivation of the Saxon word 'hereward', meaning 'steward' and this may indicate a settlement in the forest belonging to 'the steward' – possibly of the Earls of Essex. Wood has always played an important part in local history, as witness the wonderful timber work in the belfry of All Saints church, surviving bombs (in 1940) and the vagaries of weather for some 500 years.

Until recent times, surrounded as it was by rich farmlands, many being ancient manorial farms, agricultural pursuits formed the main occupation of many village inhabitants, while in the village itself the chief 'industries' were pottery, bricklaying and brickmaking. It is thought that one of Stock's claims to fame is the fact that the ancient formula for making bricks with an admixture of ashes in the clay was first used here and given the name 'Stock brick' – now universally used.

The village character is still maintained with the village green with its war memorial, the ancient windmill and many 18th century dwellings in the streets. For a long time Stock was hardly on the main road to anywhere; the arterial trunk roads (now 'A' roads) passing it by, and that helped to maintain its rural identity as a village.

There are records of a charter for a fair 'to be holden in Stok' as far back as 1239, and though not many famous personages have lived here, very many have visited, from Royalty downwards. The poet William Cowper wrote of Stock; the famous statesman William Wilberforce loved to visit here, and even today a bishop makes his home in the village. A few families are still here who can trace their residence in Stock for some 300 or 400 years.

Stondon Massey 🦌

The village of Stondon Massey is bounded on the north side by Chipping Ongar and on the south by Doddinghurst and Blackmore and has a population of 699. A brook, rising somewhat south of its centre, sweeps through the fields on the eastern side and skirts the hill leading to Stondon Hall and the parish church of St Peter and St Paul and runs into the river Roding near Ongar.

The Saxon word 'stone-don' (stoney-hill) aptly describes the gravelly summit of the hill on which the church stands. This church, built by the Normans, may have been erected on the site of a previous temple. Thin Roman bricks or tiles found in the walls suggest perhaps that Roman ruins were in the vicinity.

The Normans not only gave Stondon the church but also the additional name of 'Massey'. In 1086 the de Marcy family held land in Stondon, and it is their name that the village bears today.

In the church can be found two fine Elizabethan brasses, commemorating Rainold Hollingsworth and John Carre. The Carre brass is of particular interest as it is the only brass in England to bear the arms of the Ironmongers Company. There is a fine Jacobean pulpit and reading desk, the chancel screen dates from about 1480, and there is an impressive structure of oak beams inside the nave which supports the belfry.

Stondon Massey was the home of William Byrd, one of the greatest of English composers, who lived at Stondon Place from

1592 until his death in 1623. A memorial to his memory was erected in the parish church in 1923 and he asked in his will that he should be buried in Stondon churchyard, although it is not known exactly where his grave is. The Stondon Singers, a choir with an excellent reputation, gives a Byrd memorial concert in the church every year on or near the anniversary of his death on July 4th.

John Carre, whose brass was mentioned earlier, was also commemorated by the Giles Trust which was founded by his nephew Henry Giles. The income is still being used to help people in need in the parish, including the elderly's special needs.

There are two further trusts – the Tomlinson's Trust which was a parcel of land at Hatfield Broad Oak, the rent from which had to provide four poor widows of Stondon Massey with five shillings per annum, to be paid on the 8th of October each year. This land has now been sold and the money invested so that the charity can still be maintained. The third charity, the Bellrope, originally associated with Bellrope Cottage and used to provide bellropes for the church has a small income which is used for church repairs.

At one time there were 15 farms in the parish which, together with the manor and a few large houses, employed most of the villagers who lived in the cottages scattered around the village.

Stondon Massey's only public house, the Bricklayer's Arms, is right at the centre of the village opposite the green and the pond. The main part of the village is now just over a mile away from the church. The cause of this was probably the Black Death in 1349.

Tendring 🌿

The village of Tendring is situated between Clacton and Colchester and dates back to Saxon times. 'Tender' was an old Saxon word meaning pasture or meadow. There are few meadows now; it is mostly an arable farming area of approximately 3000 acres.

The village was the centre of the Tendring Hundred, made up of 32 villages. It still lends its name to the Tendring Peninsula, as advertised in tourist brochures.

Remains of Roman flagons and pottery have been found and there is evidence of tumuli and ancient ditches in some fields.

The Saxon church was rebuilt in the 13th century and was

dedicated to the king and martyr St Edmund. The most note-worthy feature is the hammerbeam roof, constructed 600 years ago. It is one of the remaining examples in the country. Later, a timber porch was added, and a stone tower and steeple were built in 1877, funded by John Cardinall. He was a county magistrate and landowner and lived at the manor house. During this time the population was at its peak of almost 900 inhabitants. It has since fallen to 600.

There was a small workhouse in Crown Lane. Later, the Poor Law Board gave orders for a larger establishment to serve the Tendring Hundred. In 1938 the Union House was built at a cost of £12,000. It could accommodate over 200 tramps and poor people of the area. In 1948 it became a geriatric hospital, known as Heath Hospital. The Tendring League of Friends was formed in 1961 under the chairmanship of Mr R. A. Barton, who was for many years the headmaster of the village primary school. At present there are 120 children from Tendring and surrounding villages attending the school. Opposite the church stands the old National school, built in 1842, which is now used as the village hall.

Tendring is noted for its tall, neatly clipped hedges alongside the Old Rectory and Church House. The Hall has a well-established garden, featuring magnificent azaleas and rhododendrons.

Nowadays, few people are employed on the farms but the Heath Hospital does provide some work for this small community. The village still has a post office and general stores. However, many of the residents commute to the larger towns and Tendring has become a 'dormitory' village.

Terling & Fairstead

Terling is an attractive village, steeped in history. Henry VIII had a palace here and there are many old buildings which are worth seeking out.

Amongst Terling's less obvious attributes are two local charities. Life for agricultural workers' families has never been easy. Too often they were forced to live on a diet of bread and vegetables. Until the Poor Law Act of 1834 stopped most outdoor relief many also depended on help from the Parish Overseers either in clothes or cash to make up the subsistence level wages.

In Terling they must have had an extra reason for looking forward to Christmas for thanks to the generosity of the lord of the manor and a 17th century charity there would be a joint of beef on the table and for the poorest a coat or a gown.

By the early 20th century the distribution was not dependent on 'poverty' but limited to Lord Rayleigh estate employees. It continued until 1939, ended by rationing.

The 'Bread and Beef' had become a Christmas Eve ceremony, when representatives of families converged on Terling Place to collect their 'offerings'. The church bells rang and there was quite a festive air. Pillow cases were taken along to hold the quartern loaves, and prams and box-carts, the pride of small boys to take home the spoils. Each family in turn was called out to receive its joint and loaves according to the number in family. Widows over 70 were also given flannel petticoats which sometimes had been made by the elder girls of the village school.

About 20 of those obtaining 'relief' also received from Henry Smith's Charity which still continues, though the 'Bread and Beef' is no more. Set up in 1626 for the 'relief in Clothing, Bread, Flesh and Fish for the able-bodied' this was in the hands of the overseers of the village.

The man responsible was Henry Smith, a rich London merchant and alderman. Born in Wandsworth in 1548, he died a childless widower there in 1627. From his numerous estates he left legacies to many areas through trustees. The Essex branch, which appears to have broken away from the rest, gets its money from the rent of White House Farm in Tolleshunt D'Arcy, purchased in 1635 by the Earl of Essex and fellow trustees.

How did Terling qualify? There is a local legend that Smith came disguised as a vagabond or beggar, was kindly treated and given food and clothing. At this time parishes were responsible for their own poor and were quick to rid themselves of unwanted strangers who might be a burden on the poor rate. The vicar at the time was Thomas Rust, whose predecessor had probably died from a fever brought in by a vagrant, Anne Robinson, who given shelter in a vicarage outhouse, died there. Within four months the vicar, five sons and two daughters were also dead though the cause is not registered. If true such kindness was unusual but paid off!

Between the wars the money was used to buy coal to be distributed just before Christmas and now it is paid to pensioners in cash. Few deeds of mercy can have reaped so long a reward.

Thaxted 🎵

Mention Thaxted and many people will immediately think of Morris dancing. For during the first weekend in June, the medieval streets come alive to the sound of the fiddle, tabor and fife, accordian and the jingling of bells, as the Morris Ring celebrates its annual gathering.

After a meeting held in Thaxted in 1934, attended by representatives from six of the earliest clubs, a Morris Ring was founded – a federation of Morris Teams. Since then it has become the custom for the Morris Ring to organise several gatherings every year, where men from the 250 British societies and abroad, can meet and dance together. The only Ring meeting to be held in the same place every year is in Thaxted, where the clubs used to meet even before the Ring was formed.

The exact date of the construction of Thaxted Guildhall is unknown. As there is no mention of it in the survey of 1393, it was probably built by the Guild of Cutlers, sometime between then and 1420, at a time when the cutlery industry in Thaxted was at its peak. It was sited at the meeting point of Thaxted's roads, adjacent to the market, the entrance to the manor, and the roadway to the church.

From its beginnings the Guildhall was an administrative centre. It would have been the meeting place for the Cutlers Guild and Burgesses of the Manorial Borough. Later it became the council chamber for the Mayor and Corporation, and now the parish council hold their meetings on the first floor.

Yardley's Charity was set up when Thomas Yerdele, who died in 1442 directed in his will that if his heirs died without issue, his property was to be sold and the money used to benefit the church and people of Thaxted. When his son John died childless in 1490, leaving the manor now called Yardley Farm, the inhabitants of Thaxted purchased it to establish a fund for paying the taxes levied on them by Henry VII. In 1622 the charity was regulated and new objectives added to the original benefication.

Over the centuries the charity has changed the face of Thaxted, contributing towards a hospital, the upkeep of roads, the purchase of a fire engine, the building of sewers and a school.

Today Yardley's Charity still meet in the Guildhall, as does the parish council and other organisations. Exhibitions are held

157

Thaxted Guildhall

throughout the summer, and in the autumn a produce show. The cellar housing a small museum is now open.

Theydon Bois ⚘

Theydon Bois is a village not 20 miles from the centre of London. Originally it was a hamlet in the Forest of Essex, but the coming of the railway in 1865 changed all that and it is now linked to the city by the Central Line of the Underground system. However, it still has great attraction, with its village pond on a large green which is bisected by an avenue of fine old oak trees. On the green there are still a few lovely old buildings such as the cottage formerly called Trail, now Heathfield Cottage, Baldocks and Pakes Farm.

Theydon is bordered on one side by Epping Forest and the railway line separates it from agricultural land to the south; there is a small shopping centre, a 19th century parish church, and a new Baptist church, but undoubtedly the main attraction of the village is the beautiful green, a magnet for city dwellers still in fine weather, and well remembered by those who came on Sunday school treats and outings in the past.

A life-long resident of Theydon remembers the heyday of these in the 1920s. At this time many thousands of children were brought here for a day in the country. Mostly they came from the East End of London and it was the only holiday they ever had. They came by bus and by train, long trains with many carriages – hence Theydon's long station which was built to accommodate them. From there they swarmed through the village to the forest.

'The big attractions were the "Retreats" – Grays and Yates. They were in Coppice Row, Grays opposite and Yates next to the Plain, an open green on the edge of the forest. The Retreats had swings, roundabouts helter-skelters and bicycles, the latter joined together in a circle which was pushed round by pedal power. Both Retreats had a shop where children could buy sweets, ice-creams and small presents; also very popular were rocks marked right through with the words "Theydon Bois".'

Thorpe Le Soken 🦢

Thorpe Le Soken is in the Tendring Hundred. In the neighbourhood enough things were to be found necessary for a living i.e. fresh water from a brook and wells, timber for building and fuel, fertile soil and a tidal estuary for fish. The earliest time Thorpe is mentioned is 1119 when a charter of the Abbey of St John the Baptist at Colchester refers to the tithes of Torp. In 1147 there was certainly a church, the sole relic of this building is now the font base.

Thorpe Hall has been in various hands, but the most famous was the Viscount Byng of Vimy, a former Governor General of Canada.

Thorpe has three religious meeting houses, the parish church of St Michael, the Baptist church (1801) and the Methodist church (1867). There are records of a school in Thorpe since 1648 and on 31st October 1870 the James Rolph Church of England school was opened with some 38 pupils. Still flourishing it now has approximately 185 pupils. Once having 10 public houses Thorpe now only has 5 with 3 restaurants and a cafe.

Thorpe Le Soken is a growing village with modern problems with the volume of traffic through its main street (where parking is unrestricted) heading for the coast of Walton on the Naze and Frinton on Sea.

Who was Pretty Kitty Canham? Kitty was the only daughter of Robert and Judith Canham of Thorpe. Robert was a prosperous man, living in the Tudor manor house of Beaumont Hall. In 1745 a lonely incumbent by the name of Henry Gough arrived in Thorpe. After a year's courtship, he and Kitty were married. It was a stormy marriage of bitter rows and lasted only three years, before Kitty ran off to London. There she caught the eye of a rich young man named John Primrose. The second wedding of Kitty took place in secret to avoid John's father, Lord Rosebery, serving a writ of lunacy on him!

Kitty died in Verona in 1752. On her deathbed she confessed to John that she was a bigamist and begged him to take her body home to Thorpe for burial. John set out on the journey but when the boat was searched at Brightlingsea, the finding of Kitty's embalmed body aroused the suspicions of the authorities and they arrested him. He was locked up with the coffin in the vestry of St

Leonard's church on Hythe Hill and the public flocked to see him and his strange companion. Kitty Canham's funeral was said to have been the most elaborate and costly funeral possible. From Colchester to Thorpe's St Michael's church she travelled in a handsome coffin with six large silver plates, carried by a hearse pulled by stately, black-plumed horses.

Thorrington 🦌

Thorrington is a small, but sprawling village situated between Colchester and Clacton. The name Thorrington has had many changes during the years from its first recording in the Domesday Book of 1086 as Torinduna.

Spread around the village there are five 16th century houses. The most impressive of these is Thorrington Hall which is a large farmhouse standing just north of the church, built probably shortly after St John's College, Cambridge became lords of the manor. That has obtained to the present day and the estate has been let to a series of tenant farmers who have resided in the hall.

The only remaining public house (the Red Lion) is in the middle of the parish and is a much restored and altered 17th century building.

Thorrington watermill (Coopers Mill) is, however, the most well known building. The mill, a four storeyed timber framed and boarded building, stands at the head of Alresford Creek on the outskirts of the village. It is the last surviving watermill in Essex, though it is many years since the waterwheel was turned to grind corn and when sailing barges came up the creek to the mill wharf. It has now been taken over by the Essex County Council who are restoring it with a view to getting it working again and preserving it for future generations.

The church of St Mary Magdalene stands down a lane away from the main village. The building dates from the 14th century, although there has been a small worshipping community in the parish from at least the 12th century. The most prominent feature is the fine East Anglian type knapped flint and embattled west tower, built c1480. A fine ring of six bells are still heard every Sunday – rung by a splendid and talented band of ringers.

In the mid 18th century the parish of Frating was united with that of Thorrington – and although there was a church in Frating, used until being declared redundant during the late 1970s, this has now been sold as a private dwelling.

Robert Bickersteth Mayor became rector of Frating with Thorrington in 1863, a living he held until his death in 1898. On a site in the middle of the parish, presented by St John's College, he built a school and house. The school played a most important part in the life of the parish up to the middle of the present century. He then turned his attention to the two churches, in 1866 he commenced the drastic, but necessary, restoration of Thorrington church, largely at his own expense. He also built a parsonage which became a residence for the curate, later it became the rectory, and has in recent times been replaced by a modern house. In 1870/72 he was solely responsible for the restoration and enlargement of Frating church, making it one of the prettiest little parish churches in the district.

Tilbury ✺

Tilbury is of course best known for its docks, which were built in the 1880s. However Tilbury was first known as Tulla Burgh and the Romans are known to have been in West Tilbury. Roman pottery was found in the Thames mud and an incineration burial was found at Law Street.

The Normans built a church where the present church stands in West Tilbury, but very little of their time is now left. There were five bells in the church, dating from the 17th century. William Laud built the West Tilbury rectory in 1609–1616, which had a spring said to possess healing powers.

Queen Elizabeth I made her famous speech somewhere in the vicinity of Mill House Camp, probably near Turnpike Cottages. Turnpike Cottages were one of the stagecoach stops on its way to Tilbury Fort, others being the Blue Anchor inn and the Kings Head.

Henry IV built the fort earthworks at Tilbury in 1402. Henry VIII, fearing the Papal wrath, built the blockhouse. To summon reinforcements, beacons were lit at Fobbing Hill, Beacon Hill and Langdon Hill. The fort fell into disrepair several times and was open to Dutch attacks till it was repaired by Sir Bernard de Gomme in about 1682. It is the same today, with its moat and chapel.

Tollesbury

Tollesbury's church of St Mary is well worth visiting. The chancel was rebuilt in 1872. The small octagonal font bears round the margin of the bowl 'Good people all I pray take care, that in ye Church you do not swear, as this man did'. The parish register explains the unusual warning – August 30th 1718 Elizabeth, daughter of Robert and Eliza Wood baptised in new font bought out of £5 paid by John Norman who some months before came drunk into church, cursed and talked loudly during a service.

Carved on either side of the lectern is a plough and sailing ship, symbolic of two kinds of work which engaged most of the male population. This has been the symbol to this day of Tollesbury.

Tollesbury achieved fame as a yachting centre, yachts from Tollesbury sailing round the world. Tollesbury mariners sailed in the Royal yacht *Britannia*, one time skippered by Charles Leavett, and a number contended in the America's Cup races.

There were four oyster packing houses on the saltings. In 1876–7 Tollesbury and Mersea (Blackwater) Oyster Fisher Co (Ltd) was formed. Its aim was to give protection to men and oysters. This was in the time when men's only way of providing for their families was through their work, no work meant no money.

Herons, tern and shelduck at Tollesbury

163

Other forms of fishing roundabout Tollesbury included 'Five Fingering' ie catching starfish. These starfish would be used on farms for manure or perhaps go to Colchester for distribution. Winkles and eels were also sought after.

On October 1st 1904 the Crab and Winkle Express ran from Kelvedon low level railway station on its nine miles journey to Tollesbury. The Crab and Winkle faithfully served on this same line for 47 years.

The railway was revived during the Second World War when the War Department took over the derelict Tollesbury Pier Extension as part of the defence system against invasion. The Kelvedon and Tollesbury Light Railway fought a valiant war, ferrying troops to the coastal defence batteries and carrying mobile anti-aircraft guns.

Farming was one of the main occupations for the male population. Women obviously worked during picking seasons such as peas, beans and potatoes.

Tollesbury is a village used by boat lovers, boasting a marina and a Sailing Club. Now workers commute to towns although some light industry has flourished. It has remained a popular village, newcomers always finding friendly faces and a welcome.

Tolleshunt D'Arcy

Tolleshunt D'Arcy is an attractive village situated on the Blackwater estuary. The word Tolleshunt comes from the Anglo Saxon 'Tolleshunta' which means 'Toll's spring'. It is thought Toll was an Anglo Saxon chief who settled large areas of forest, establishing clearings where water was readily available. Neighbouring parishes are Tolleshunt Major and Tolleshunt Knights.

At the time of the Domesday survey Tolleshunta was known to have a number of salt pans. Salt is still retrieved from the river at nearby Maldon. This salt is justly famous and exported to many countries of the world.

William the Conqueror gave the manor to Ralph Peverell for services rendered during the Conquest. The later part of the village name altered as female heirs changed the name to that of their husbands. It became in turn, Tolleshunt Tregoz, Tolleshunt Valoines and Tolleshunt de Boys. John D'Arcy married a daughter of the de Boys family. By this match the estate came to the D'Arcy family in the 1400s. It remained in the family until the death of Thomas D'Arcy in 1593.

During that period D'Arcy Hall was built as the family home. A splendid early 16th century building which still remains. Inside is some fine panelling bearing Anthony D'Arcy's initials and the date 1540. A bridge spanning the moat dates from the Elizabethan period as does the dovecote in the grounds. The russet D'Arcy Spice apple originated from these gardens in 1840.

At the heart of the village stands the Maypole. This is a 'listed building' of indeterminate age, but believed locally to be one of less than a handful of genuine Maypoles remaining in the country. It is now protected by a wooden cage.

In close proximity to the Maypole is D'Arcy House. A well proportioned Queen Anne style dwelling this has been the home at different periods of two of Tolleshunt D'Arcy's most famous residents.

It was the home of Dr John Salter from 1864 to 1932. Born in 1841, the eldest son of a country gentleman, he had a long and varied career. The Doctor was a prize winning horticulturist, Vice-President of the English Kennel Club, and in his 70s he became Provincial Grand Master of the Freemasons. He will probably be best remembered for his diary which he kept from 1849 until 1932.

Later the house became the home of well known author Margery Allingham, creator of the fictional detective Albert Campion, and her husband Lt Col Philip Youngman Carter. He was a skilled illustrator who followed up a spell spent as Features Editor for the *Daily Express* with ten years in the Editor's chair at the *Tatler*.

Although the village has long since lost its single track railway known as the 'Crab and Winkle' line, it is regularly served by Osborne's Bus Company. This small friendly, privately run company was founded in 1918, offering a personal service. It still remains predominantly staffed by members of the Osborne family.

Important features of village life are usually its church and public houses. Tolleshunt D'Arcy can boast of having both a church and chapel, plus five public houses within the parish. The parish church of St Nicholas is in the Perpendicular style with a west tower, and a nave ceiling which was decorated in 1897 by Ernest Geldart.

Tolleshunt Knights 🪶

There are many stories and legends connected with the history of Tolleshunt Knights. Barnhall appears to be the subject of the best known legend, though there are very many variations. The tale has been recorded both in prose and verse.

It is the tale of the celebrated 'Virley Devil' who objected to the start of building in the Devils Wood when he challenged the workman who had been left to guard the site that night. In answer to Satan's cry of 'Who is there' the workman replied 'God, myself and my three spey bitches' and the Devil went away. This was repeated on the second night. However, when the Devil made his challenge on the third night the man answered 'Myself, my three spey bitches and God'. He had put it the wrong way round, so the devil reached out his claws and tore the heart out of the man's body. He took a beam from the house and threw it up the hill saying

> 'Where this beam shall fall
> There shall ye build Barnhall'

The watchman's heart was reputed to have been buried in the wall of the old Bushes church at Tolleshunt Knights and the beam with Satan's claw marks is still visible in the cellar of Barnhall.

Of great interest to lovers of local history is the effigy of a knight in the old Bushes church. This knight was probably Sir John Atte Lee, he is shown in armour of about 1380. He wears a helmet called a bascinet and in his hands he holds a heart. The lower part of the tomb on which the figure lay came to light in 1953.

The present day life of the village is very varied with a great mixture of residents who have spent most of their lives in the area and are fully versed with all its history, and newcomers who have settled in Tolleshunt Knights and are just as interested in its past.

The well known and very active St John the Baptist Monastery is situated in Rectory Road, as is the famous Hylands Farm, home of the Whitehouse Ivy nurseries. Many of the ivies produced here have the title 'Knights' in their name.

Toot Hill 🌿

Toot Hill is one of the small hamlets that make up the parish of Stanford Rivers. The shop and post office have been closed and it is now purely a residential area, with the old coaching inn, the Green Man, attracting many visitors.

One of the landmarks of Toot Hill was the windmill, which could be seen from a great distance. It was built about 1824 and was the property of Mr Edward Rayner who leased it to the miller Mr Joseph Knight. The windmill became notorious due to a storm that struck it on Thursday 18th June 1829. The electrical charge which virtually destroyed the mill, was so great that it was actually commented on in the national *Mechanics Magazine*! Mr Knight, who was working at the time, was severely scorched, and one of his legs was so badly fractured that it had to be amputated. The locals were so shocked that a petition was drawn up on behalf of the miller and his family and lodged at the Green Man. A line drawing of the mill was made by Isaac Taylor and the prints were sold 'for Joseph Knight and his family consisting of a wife and seven children one of whom is deaf and dumb' at 2d each.

The mill was renovated and put to use again, and remained in use until 1910 when it was again struck by lightning. It was damaged once more by fire in 1928 and finally demolished in 1935. Little can be seen of its site today.

Toppesfield 🌿

Windy Toppesfield straddles the top of a 300 foot hill, two miles from the main trunk road from Cambridge to Harwich. Gainsford End is the sister village, on high ground on the far side of the valley. Though the old pub The Wheatsheaf is closed, Gainsford End can now boast of a fine museum devoted to the working horse, an animal sanctuary and the ruined windmill.

The Causeway climbs gently past one of the few remaining thatched cottages left after many were demolished in the 1950s, past Toppesfield House, until recently the rectory and where a thatched tithe barn once stood, and past a magnificent row of pink flowering horse chestnut trees. Here an avenue leads to the

17th century manor house of Berwick Hall, once the home of Lord and Lady Plummer, who encouraged the fund raising for the village hall, among other good works.

Toppesfield Stores, formerly a bakery and stores, the post office formerly another bakery, two public houses – The Chestnut and The Green Man, and the Congregational chapel are all to be found in The Street. Beside the chapel is another thatched cottage and in the centre of the wide road junction is a roofed structure on pillars called 'the pumps', erected to celebrate Queen Victoria's Diamond Jubilee.

A deep pond opposite the stores in front of the blacksmith's shop, brick lined and fenced, has been filled in to allow access to a close of modern bungalows built on the grounds of ancient Camoise manor. A footpath leads to the churchyard.

The church of St Margaret of Antioch, built in the 14th century of plastered flint rubble, has a red brick tower, built in 1699 after the original tower collapsed. The chancel is built at a slight angle to the nave. There is a gallery, a little ancient stained glass, and a brass mostly hidden by the organ, of John and Agnes Cracherode 1534. The organ also hides the 13th century marble statue of a knight, Thomas le Despenser who occupied the manor of 'Camoys'.

In Stambourne Road there is a terrace of 'Improved Farm-workers Dwellings' dating from the 1870s with a characteristic text carving. Further down Stambourne Road is another thatched property.

Past inhabitants of the village include Samuel Symonds of 'Olivers' who went to Massachusetts in 1637 to become Deputy Governor, responsible for Topsfield, Massachusetts.

Ugley ✥

Ugley – a name to conjure with! and surely the magic of the place must have cast a spell on the Norseman, Ugga as he made his little clearing or ley in this part of the great East Anglian forest.

Bluebell woods still surround the 'ley' and here and there the huge puddingstones, glacial deposits of some 150–180 million years ago, bob up as markers, some say, for the route of medieval pilgrims.

St Peter's church stands well to the north-east, isolated except for the Hall and a farmhouse. Part of the church is 13th century but an earlier church at Bollington, now a hamlet, and belonging to King Harold was re-erected when in ruins as a chapel on the south side of St Peter's. The church was enlarged with a west tower in the 16th century and re-built with additions in the 19th century.

Of the ancient charitable trusts, the Buck family of Bollington Hall who were haberdashers and drapers left bequests in 1558 for providing suits or materials for three poor men and women, but Robert Buck in 1620 specified that the gifts were to be 'sheepskins and an ell of roan canvas' and for the women 'fustian for bodices and sack-cloth for petty-coats'. With a legacy from Edward Sandford in 1863 (for coal or clothing) these two trusts now bring in £48 annually, distributed as money.

Sarah Chamberlayne, born at Orford House, left in 1858 a sum to be paid yearly to several villages and for land to be bought for almshouses for 5 poor persons in Ugley. But no land became available, so trustees were appointed to enable eight people to receive £7 quarterly.

Halfway from London to Newmarket, on the old Epping road, Orford House at Ugley was said to be a convenient overnight stop for Charles II on his way to the races. Now in the hands of the Home Farm Trust, 'Orford' gives a home, work and a settled future to some 20 young handicapped men and women.

1941 and the Second World War saw bombs fall on the village hall, the Tennant family's Great War memorial for Ugley. Now, a vigorous hall committee keeps the restored building in fine shape.

Legends and traditions carry on. The 'Pharisees (fairies?) Hole' is said to lie half-way in a passage connecting Ugley Hall with Rickling Hall a mile away – both on ancient sites. A groom in the stable at Ugley declared he could hear a coach passing half a mile away as it crossed the subsidence in the old Cambridge Road known as the Pharisees Hole. And at Rickling Hall the sound of falling bricks comes through the tunnel – from that hole half a mile away.

Upminster ✒

Upminster has a very long history; the centre of the town where there are traffic lights is the site of very old trackways. The crossroads also mark what was once the centre of the village green where stood the Bell, now remembered in name only, it having been replaced by shops and a travel agency.

For the best part of 800 years Upminster was divided roughly into two manors. The northern area (later Upminster Hall manor) was granted by Earl Harold to the abbey he founded at Waltham, where it remained until the dissolution of the monasteries. Eventually in 1685 it came into the possession of the Branfills. The last Branfill to live at the manor died in 1890, leaving a son of only 2½ years. With the coming of the steam railway shortly after, the relatives started to sell the estate, which marked the beginning of the development of Upminster as a middle class residential suburb. Upminster Hall still stands and is owned by the Upminster Golf Club.

Gaynes manor to the south has a much more complicated history. Important to Upminster were the last owners, the Esdailes. However, in 1839 the estate passed out of their hands and was broken up. Some buildings still remain and a part of the parkland, but the mansion was demolished after it had been built only 50 years.

Facing what was the Bell is St Laurence's church. It is believed a church was here before the Conquest, as Upminster which means the church on the hill is mentioned in the Domesday Book. The present church had its beginnings in the 13th century, but had many additions and alterations after that, and in 1862 was completely renovated. There still remain some interesting old brasses and a piece of medieval glass with the Engayne, Latham and Deyncourt arms (all past owners of Gaynes manor) thereon, and what appears to be part of a garden scene.

Buried in St Laurence's church in 1400, leaving some money to the parish was the notorious woman Alice Perrers, one time mistress of Edward III. She became lord of the manor of Gaynes through her marriage to Sir William Windsore.

A well known landmark is the fine windmill. Surprisingly it was not built until 1803. It is a smock mill, one of only two in Essex (the other is at Terling). Up to the late 1950s it was falling into a state of decay, but happily since then a band of enthusiasts have restored it (it has lately undergone further renovation) and it is opened a few times a year to the public.

There are still some houses standing of the old Upminster, notably Great Tomkyns a 15th century house, and an old tithe barn, but many have disappeared even since the last history was written in 1962. Upminster has multiplied four fold since the war but fortunately for Upminster what was once church glebe land was bought by a far-seeing Council in 1929 for a recreation ground which means that down one side of the main road there is still an open space.

Upshire 🐝

Upshire lies on the outskirts of Epping Forest between Waltham Abbey and Epping. It comprises two hamlets, Upshire or Upstra – which means 'hilly road' – and Copt Hall Green (Copt means 'top of a hill'). Its traceable history goes back to the Iron Age, when the earthworks known as Ambresbury Banks were constructed. Legend has it that Boadicea mustered her army there for her last battle against the Romans at nearby Nazeing. Two 18th century obelisks, standing about a mile apart, are supposed to mark the spots where she took poison and died.

The oldest building is probably Upshire Hall, which is believed to be medieval. It is a listed building and it contains a window pane which is ornamented by the signature of the Prince Regent. Most other houses date from the 18th century onwards and there is a small council housing estate, with its own parade of shops and a large mobile homes site. Other buildings include a church, a primary school, a village hall and two pubs. The village post office and general stores closed some years ago.

For over a hundred years, Upshire was home to the Buxton family (of Truman, Hanbury and Buxton, the brewers). They lived first at Warlies Park and then at Woodredon House. Warlies once belonged to Samuel Foxe, son of John Foxe of *Foxe's Book of Martyrs* fame. Latterly, it became a Dr Barnardo's Home and is now owned by the Conservators of Epping Forest, who let it out as office space. They also own Woodredon, which is now a home for mentally handicapped adults. The Buxtons were active in many areas of social reform and education.

Anyone who has driven on the M25 past the Waltham Abbey turn off will have noticed Copped Hall. It is an 18th century mansion which, from a distance, looks beautiful. Close to, it is a nightmare! The windows, roof and inside walls all disappeared in a fire in 1917. The outside walls are protected by a preservation order and, over the years, there have been various ideas for restoring the house.

Sir Winston Churchill was often seen in Upshire when he was a guest of Sir Herbert and Lady Llewellyn Smith, who lived nearby. Perhaps his artist's eye was caught by the 'Blue Row', a row of white weatherboarded cottages with blue front doors.

Present day Upshire is struggling to come to terms with the effect of having the M25 driven straight through it. Despite the constant noise. Upshire has become a more desirable place to live because of its proximity to two motorways.

Many Upshire people, like their forbears, work on the land. Some are farmers, some work for the Conservators of Epping Forest and others at local riding establishments. The remainder follow a multiplicity of trades and professions. Living in Epping Forest gives them the rights to gather fallen wood and to graze cattle in the forest.

Vange ෨ᢒ

Since Saxon times Vange has had many different spellings of its name. The Domesday Book records it as having two manors, that later became united into one. In 1953 a Bronze Age hoard was found in the grounds of Swan Mead School, and a coin of Emperor Gratian, AD 375–378 was found at Merricks Farm.

Clement Dawes is stated to have farmed the land at Vange Hall in 1581. The hall was extended in the 19th century and had a large cellar, dairy and 20 rooms. In 1886 the owner, Mr R. Curtis, discovered two hidden rooms in the roof with boarded floors, nails and hooks for clothes. It is thought they were probably used as hiding places for Catholic priests in Elizabethan times.

Vange also contains a number of pubs, the Five Bells being built during the middle to late 1600s, it is also reputed to have its own ghost. In days gone by inquests were carried out at the Barge Inn, and the stables were used as a mortuary!

In the early 1920s an advert appeared for 'Vange Water – cures all ills'. This natural spring water came from Cash's Farm and was bottled and then sold for medicinal purposes, one wine glassful being the stated dosage. This did not last for long, but for a while people came from near and far to taste this spring water in the hope of a miraculous cure.

All Saints Church has parts dating back to the 11th and 12th centuries, the nave is reputed to be late 11th century. Customs of Vange are few and far between, but it is noted that in 1503, the body of John Sawnder was carried to Vange churchyard for burial and before it was driven a sheep. Apparently, this medieval custom was known as the foredrove, an offering at death of an animal or animals to the church, which were driven before the funeral procession and was peculiar to this part of England.

At the beginning of this century land plots were sold off to Londoners, who commuted down by train at weekends to build small weekend bungalows to live in for their holidays. Plots at Vange 20 feet × 100 feet were advertised and sold for approximately £5 each, a lot cheaper than todays prices!

In the 1970s one of Vange's country houses built in 1420 was sacrificed to provide a gypsy camp in Burnt Mills Vange. The majority of the Old Vange Village has now been swallowed up by the development of Basildon New Town, but memories still linger.

Weeley ❦

Living in the village of Weeley is a family of the same name and their family tree goes back to the days when the head of the family was the lord of the manor.

It may be unusual to find a family living in a village of the same name, but this was more by design than accident. After the Civil War the manor of Weeley was up for sale and a Doctor William Weoley, from London, bought the estate. The village was then known as Weeleigh and in old documents there have been found to be no less than 39 variations of the spelling. William Weoley changed his name to Weeley and soon ensured that the name of the village was identical.

William's family came from Camden, Gloucestershire, and were granted a coat of arms which the present family are still entitled to use.

Weeley has never been noted for its growth. At the time of the Domesday Book there were 11 tenants, 9 smallholders and 4 serfs, who together with their families made up about 120 persons. By the year 1801 the census showed that the population had grown to only 387 and today it still numbers only about 1700.

The largest number of people ever to gather in Weeley was in August 1971 when the first big 'pop' festival was held. An estimated 100,000 people from many parts of the world gathered here for the weekend event.

Wendens Ambo 🌿

Originally there were two villages, Wenden Magna and Wenden Parva, whose churches were only half a mile apart, but after the Restoration both became very impoverished and the joint income could scarcely provide a living for just one minister. So it was that in 1662, by an Instrument issued under the Episcopal Seal of the Bishop of London, that Wendens Ambo was created, the name meaning the Wendens together. Only the church of Wenden Magna was retained and the rectory of Wenden Parva became the vicarage of the new parish.

Twenty or so years ago Wendens Ambo was referred to as the 'dying village' as there were only about 40–50 children out of a population of about 350. Not so today, however, as there are about 150 children without any great increase in the number of houses. Audley End railway station is a very good reason for some

Audley End House near Wendens Ambo

residents having come to the village as they can walk to it to get to work in London, Cambridge and Harlow.

Before the village became 'sought after' the three farms within its bounds and the railway were the main employers of labour. However, with modernisation the three farms and railway now employ few people, and the shop has gone, but the occupations of the residents are now many and varied.

The parish hall, church and The Bell are the main meeting points. The hall, a modest building of red brick built in 1838, is the venue for many of the activities and in recent years has been much improved by local effort.

The most important building in the village is the church, with the oldest parts dating from the 11th century, which is often pictured in guidebooks and calendars with the attractive old cottages leading up to it. On the farm next to the church is a thatched barn reputed to be the largest in England. In all there are 17 Grade II buildings, but among them will not be found the fine Elizabethan house in Duck Street. In fact it came from Suffolk in 1939 as the owner wanted to live nearer London! It was reassembled meticulously as all the timbers had been numbered and then rejoined with wooden pegs, no nails.

Before the M11 was built through the western part of the village the Department of Archaeology at Cambridge University in 1973 carried out a dig which revealed a Roman site, which was known about, and also the remains of an Iron Age settlement of the period 300–200 BC.

West Bergholt ✤

West Bergholt is reputed to mean 'a wood on a hill' and an investigation carried out by the local Workers' Educational Association in 1985 established certain wooded areas as being 3000 years old. Various 'finds' over the years of coins and traces of Roman roads indicate that there were Roman settlements in the vicinity.

Records recall that the village has always been an industrial area as there were mills before the Norman Conquest. From the 14th century they were used as 'fulling mills' in connection with the cloth making process, and as this trade declined they were converted into corn and oil mills. Properties stand on those same sites today bearing the original names of Cooks Mill and Newbridge Mill. There was also a working windmill. 'Horsepits' is an early 16th century timber framed building and was built by a cloth merchant as his home. A secret room has been discovered revealing the date 1628 and the initials DTS.

There is evidence of brickmaking dating back to 1570. Many local field names relate to the trade and a kiln was recently excavated.

Agriculture and farming were the main source of employment until the founding of a family brewing business by Thomas Daniell in 1820. This greatly altered the environment of the village because, as the business grew and prospered, houses were built for the workers, which increased the population and created a general expansion. The brewery remained the hub of village life until its closure in the early 1980s.

St Mary's Old Church, which is now redundant, dates from before the Norman Conquest and a wall painting that was uncovered in 1986 depicts the Royal Coat of Arms of James I and is dated 1605.

During the reign of Queen Mary, when Catholicism was in favour, there were two martyrs. Richard George's wife, Agnes, who was a Protestant was burnt at the stake at Stratford in London in 1556 for failing to attend church. His second wife was also burnt, in the grounds of Colchester Castle. He himself was imprisoned.

A philanthropist by the name of Thomas Love who died in 1565 left a legacy of £120 to buy land, the rent from which was to go to the poor of several parishes. West Bergholt was one such beneficiary and is still in receipt of money today. In 1836 three to eight yards of calico was given to the poor depending on the size of their families. Oral tradition states that Mr Love visited neighbouring parishes disguised as a beggar and those who treated him well were included in the bequest, others were sent a whip.

During the 1850s a body of agricultural workers became known as 'the fire raisers' for starting nine fires as a protest against low wages and the introduction of farm machinery. West Bergholt was called 'the most ignorant village in the county' and it was suggested that the only way to stop the fires and riots was to get the people back to church and to provide schools to educate the young to 'better ways'. The present school was built in 1858 on the heathland by the Church of England.

West Mersea 🐚

West Mersea is on the Island of Mersea and is sometimes cut off from the mainland by the only road when the tide is high. The origin of the name Mersea was Meres-ig, the Island of Mere and the West is merely to differentiate it from East Mersea.

The heart of the village is centred around the lovely old church of St Peter and St Paul. It is believed that the first church was built on Roman foundations in the late 7th or 8th century. It was rebuilt in the mid 10th century and the base of the present tower probably dates from this building. It is here in the centre that we find most of the shops, library, banks etc, but there are also shops dotted about the village, often rubbing shoulders with houses, just as the old cottages do with the new houses. Perhaps it is this hodge-podge which gives the village its charm, for charm it most certainly has.

It is not surprising, since it is so near to Colchester, to learn that there are Roman mosaics to be found but the most famous Roman relic is undoubtedly the Barrow, a Roman burial mound believed

Oysters at West Mersea

178

to have been erected in the 1st century AD, which is situated beside the East Mersea Road.

In the past farming and fishing (not to mention the famous oyster beds) were the main occupations and there is more than a suspicion that in days gone by some of the inhabitants of Mersea, like those of many of the villages round the estuary, were engaged in smuggling. There is still a small fishing fleet and of course there are still farms. It is a haven for yachtsmen and there is a flourishing Yacht Club. Wind-surfing and water-skiing are popular sports.

The village appears to have had more than its share of hauntings. By Barrow Hill the sound of heavy wheels and horses have been heard for generations and a retired schoolmaster recalls the time when, with a car full of children, the apparition of a Roman chariot and horses appeared across the bonnet. In the Lane, the oldest part of Mersea, ghostly footsteps are heard in the bedroom of the cottage where the rector, hundreds of years ago, murdered his ne'er-do-well son and then hanged himself in remorse. The happy laughter of a Roman lady friend of Claudius with whom she spent weekends, but who was drowned during a midnight swim, is still heard at West Mersea Hall, which is built on the site of a Roman villa!

Wethersfield ༻

In 1806 a young man arrived in Wethersfield to take up the position of curate. That man was none other than Patrick Bronte who was later to move to Yorkshire and father a son, Branwell and three famous daughters, Emily, Anne and Charlotte. During his three year stay in the village, however, love blossomed. He experienced a romantic courtship with his first love, a local girl, Mary Burden. But this was not to last and he moved away taking an alternative curacy in Shropshire.

The register of the parish church of St Mary Magdalene records his stay. This building, standing proudly on the hill dates in part from Norman times with its massive 28 foot square tower erected in about the year 1200. The visit of another famous figure is remembered in a small stained glass lozenge in a south side window. It depicts a symbol of Anne Boleyn, famous wife of

179

Henry VIII. The bells of this historic building ring out loud and clear across the village.

The village, situated only nine miles from Braintree, is far from dependent on its local town, being equipped with its own post office, butcher, DIY store, baker and general stores, as well as a primary school, police station, doctors' surgery and smart new fire station, built to replace the wooden shed used until 1983 which remains on the road out of the village towards Finchingfield, the village's famous neighbour.

Any commentary on Wethersfield, however short, cannot go without mention of the USAF air base, which houses servicemen of the Red Horse runway repair unit and also serves to supply a number of the village population with employment.

Of its name, it is believed that Wethersfield stems from Wutha, the name of a Viking-Scandinavian sea raider who, in the 8th–10th centuries, tramped from Mersea, up the valley of the river Pant and made a clearing in an ancient forest thus creating 'Wuths' feld' (Saxon clearing or field).

A typical village cricket scene

Wicken Bonhunt 🙢

Wicken Bonhunt comprises two small Domesday hamlets – Wica and Banhunta. The latter, at a bend of the B1038 about a mile from the main village towards Newport, where the M11 crosses the road, now consists of two houses and a farm (converted to a private house) together with a tiny Saxon or very early Norman chapel, which was for many years used as a barn. This was the church of St Helen, once attached to the manor of Bonhunt, and is by far the oldest building in the district.

Wicken, the main part of the village, sprawls along the road, which here follows the stream known as Wicken Water. Now dry for most of the year, with its bed becoming overgrown with grass and weeds, 30 years ago it ran with a foot or two of water all year round.

Behind the pub is the small village church. While a church has stood on this site since the 11th century all that remains of this structure is the massive Norman font. Most of the church you see today dates effectively from Victorian times, when the ruinous state of the building necessitated such extensive repairs that it amounted to a virtual rebuilding. Fortunately the village had at that time a wealthy vicar who footed most of the bill, and at the same time built himself the massive vicarage, in the Victorian Gothic taste.

It was probably at the time of this renovation that the ancient custom of the curfew was reintroduced – the nightly ringing of the 8.00 bell to remind villagers that bedtime was drawing near. This continued, with a break during the Second World War, down to the mid 1960s, and was only abandoned then because no-one could be found to replace the retiring verger, George Goodwin MM, whose job it had been for many years. George was one of those chosen to receive the Royal Maundy money when the Queen distributed this annual charity at Chelmsford Cathedral.

The village bakery, where bread was baked daily in real wood fired ovens, closed in 1963; the building lay empty for some years, but then a thriving signwriting business took over the premises, which has been rebuilt into an impressive works employing over a score of people, some from the village.

Behind the church is Wicken Hall, the main manor of the village to which the largest farm was at one time attached. The most interesting house in the village is Brick House built in about 1602 for the Bradbury family. Though in those days a brick house was a bit of a novelty – the usual in these parts being lath and plaster on a timber frame – the bricks used were secondhand. It has recently been found that most of the bricks had been 'turned' with their weathered faces inward to preserve the outward appearance of the house. The ancient tithe barn attached has also recently been converted into a private house of unusual design.

Altogether a very pleasant village, and one well worth a stop at the Coach and Horses. The gantry pub sign, a speciality of the local brewery, has been repainted and the faces of the passengers in the coach are taken from cartoon sketches of village characters past and present, whose originals, by Gill Potter, adorn the walls of the public bar.

Widdington 🌿

On a hill in north west Essex only a stone's throw from the bustling M11 is the small village of Widdington, many of its older buildings built around or near its attractive green. At one time it was a quiet backwater but now visitors frequent it to see the fine restored 14th century Priors Hall Barn and the Wildlife Park at Mole Hall.

Our ancestors in the village seem to have been quite lethargic with regard to their church building of St Mary's, for in 1594 it was reported to be 'in decay', in 1686 the 'tower was crackt' and consequently on 15th May 1771 the whole steeple fell down! In Victorian times the present tower was built and the church was re-opened in 1873, and thanks to present day villagers the church clock strikes the hour, the bells ring out on suitable occasions and the flag flies vigorously on its sturdy pole.

The long front gardens of the cottages in the High Street originated when a public spirited Victorian built a row of substantial cottages behind the delapidated ones near the road and the latter were then demolished.

Some of the older inhabitants recall the days when there was a village band and a ladies cricket team, and the children attended the Church school where as many as 90 pupils, some with clogs muddied from walking across the fields, were educated in two classrooms.

There is no record of Widdington having a Maypole, but there is an equally lovely custom the children used to take part in as late as 1960. The children would decorate two hoops with flowers and leaves, held together in the middle with a small dressed doll. No one now remembers what the doll represented. Some authorities state that the doll may have represented Flora, the Goddess of Spring. Two children would carry the garland through the village, followed by their school mates carrying bunches of flowers.

The well known artist Sir G. Clauson RA lived in Widdington with his family at a house called 'Bishops'. Many of his paintings can be seen in the illustrated *Larkrise to Candleford*. On leaving the village in 1905, Mr G. Clauson as he was then, gave his studio to the village to be used as a parish room and reading room, later to be known as Widdington Men's Club.

Willingale 🌿

Within ten miles due west of the county town of Chelmsford can be found the villages of Willingale Spain and Willingale Doe. Set in the heart of fine Essex farmland, the 500 or so members of Willingale's population enjoy more than their fair share of the tranquillity of rural life.

The rare historical feature to be discovered in Willingale is the sight of two well preserved churches standing side by side in the same churchyard. Legend has it that two sisters, quarrelling about their own individual rights, settled the dispute, simply, by building a church each. Since the churches were built 200 years apart, this can hardly be true but, like all good village legends, there are many who prefer it to the truth.

The village names are taken from the post-Norman Conquest landowners. Hervey d'Espana and William D'Ou. The older church of St Andrew, has a spire and dates back to the 12th century. It is now only used on Palm Sunday when the palms are blessed before a procession is made to the newer church of St Christopher. Its tower stands majestically as the focal point of the village and can be seen from all the approaches to Willingale. From the rear of the churchyard, one can savour splendidly picturesque views of the Roding valley and beyond.

Willingale has not, however, always been a picture of peace and tranquillity. A Class A airfield was built here between 1942 and 1943 by the 831st Engineer Battalion (Aviation) of the US Army. It became the home of the 387th Bomb Group of the US Eighth Air Force's 4th (subsequently 3rd) Bomb Wing. Operations began on 15th August, 1943 with B-26 Marauders. On one of the early missions, 55 B-26s took off virtually blind in early morning mist. One aircraft crashed at the end of the runway killing all but the tail gunner. The 387th remained at Willingale until July, 1944. Evidence of this brief but significant moment in Willingale's history can still be found in remnants of the perimeter track and a number of buildings.

Things may not be quite what they were in the days of thriving shops and a busy blacksmith. But you can still hear the gentle sound of leather on willow as 22 men in white compete on the village cricket green on a summer afternoon and then you feel that, perhaps, things have not changed so much after all.

Wivenhoe ✒️

Wivenhoe until recently, has always lived by the river; fishing, boat building and smuggling – not necessarily in that order! Boat building and its attendant trades of carpentry, sail and ropemaking was a thriving industry. One famous shipbuilder, Philip Sainty, combined his talent for shipbuilding with an equal talent for smuggling – he used his knowledge of building fast yachts for the well-to-do to build fast get-away boats for smugglers.

The Ropery was situated at The Cross and prospered until the First World War. The 'rope walk' is remembered by not-so-old residents, as a deep ditch running from the works, down The Avenue as far as Harvey Road. The large yachts which were crewed and skippered by Wivenhoe men, were laid up in the river for the winter, then re-commissioned, painted and provisioned in the spring. They, or their owners, did not survive the war, so, its trade diminished, the Ropery closed.

Fishing for sprats, shrimps and oysters provided a living for residents; also for the crews of the large yachts who were paid off when their ship was laid up in the river for the winter, and had to sustain themselves and their families until spring, when, hopefully, they were re-employed. There was a fish canning business on the quay until recently. Now, since fishing has practically ceased, and the shipyards are closed (one, Wivenhoe Port is about to suffer a change of use) Wivenhoe has become a dormitory for London and Colchester.

The church of St Mary the Virgin dates back to the 11th–12th century and is a mixture of building materials. The tower is of dressed flints, with stone framing. In the chancel floor are two brasses; one of William, Viscount Beaumont, one of Elizabeth, his wife, and in the sanctuary a small brass of Sir Thomas Westley, Elizabeth's chaplain. William Beaumont became insane and was cared for by his friend, the Earl of Oxford at Wivenhoe Hall (long since gone, replaced by the George V playing field).

One notable building, in East Street, is the Garrison House, the best example of pargetting in Europe. It derives its name from the Roundhead troops stationed there during the Siege of Colchester, 1648. It is now being restored, and two pictures, a cartouche upstairs and a rural scene downstairs have been retained. Other paintings in the house have been photographed and recorded.

Wivenhoe Park, subject of Constable's painting, is still extant, although overwhelmed and diminished by the blue brick tower blocks and concrete and glass buildings of Essex University.

Woodham Ferrers & Bicknacre

Woodham Ferrers is situated on a hilly site, some nine miles south east of Chelmsford and seven miles south west of Maldon. It is mentioned in the 1086 Domesday Book as Udeham, which translated means a settlement in a wood. The village and surrounding area was given to Henry de Ferrieres, hence the 'Ferrers' (or, as is sometimes used, Ferris) in the village name.

Today Woodham Ferrers is a quiet rural village surrounded by farms of both arable and mixed types. It overlooks the old boggy marshes which were once part of the parish and which are now known as South Woodham Ferrers (now duly drained). However, it was not always so quiet, as in 1338 a charter was granted for a Thursday market and a Michaelmas Fair, and old documents mention six butchers' shops, a brewery, sundry alehouses, many old houses and a workhouse, practically all of which have disappeared.

Archbishop Sandys (a forefather of the present large Sandys family) had a family home in the 16th century in the village, in the Tudor mansion of Edwins Hall.

Bicknacre too is a very old settlement, Saxon in origin, the name being derived from Bicca (possibly the name of the tribe or the tribal chief who lived here) and acre, the Saxon word for a cultivated clearing. It was essentially a meeting of roads and tracks and a drovers' resting place on the Common or Hooe.

Most of the land would have been owned by the manor of Bicknacre Priory. This priory was originally a hermitage and was occupied at least as early as 1156. It was used by Augustinian canons and although fairly well endowed to begin with, it was never a very wealthy establishment. It was, however, a resting place for pilgrims, the next available place of hospitality being Leez Priory.

In Moor Hall Lane until recently there was the Hospital and Homes of St Giles, which was the last hospital for leprosy sufferers in Great Britain, and further along the lane is their cemetery for the nuns who nursed the patients and the sufferers also. The hospital was closed in 1983 as modern medicine can now arrest the progress of leprosy and an isolated home for patients is not needed.

After being, for many years, a very small hamlet, Bicknacre, in the last 20 years has grown out of all proportion. There has been a lot of estate building and with it a new school and shops. Woodham Ferrers, the old market town, has shrunk, Bicknacre, the hamlet, has grown and grown and has now hopefully reached its majority.

Wormingford 🦋

The village was part of the land owned by Earl Godwin (King Harold's father) and after the conquest it was divided into four manors, Garnons (mentioned in Domesday), Woodhall, Church Hall and Wormingford Hall. These, together with the Grove, the Grange and Rotchfords, still lie within the parish. The manor houses, built mostly in Tudor and Stuart times, have great character and are still inhabited. Some families have lived there for many generations, particularly the Tufnells and the Boggis-Rolfes who are an embodiment of the tradition of patronage of church and school.

The main feature of the village is St Andrew's church which dates from the 12th century. It commands a magnificent view of the Stour valley and this part of the parish is in the Dedham Vale Conservation Area. There are tombs of some of the Constable family in the churchyard and there is also the grave of John Nash, the painter who lived in the village over 50 years until his death in 1977.

Although dedicated to St Andrew the church has a stained glass window depicting St George slaying the dragon. It is a modern window given in gratitude for those returning from the Second World War but it also commemorates the Wormingford dragon. It may be significant that the name of the village changed to Wormingford in the Middle Ages and Worm was the name for a dragon!

There is another glass window of historical interest in Church Hall, a 16th century Tudor rose roundall which commemorates the visit to the house of Queen Elizabeth I in 1561.

In the Second World War Wormingford was host to the USAAF but the airfield has now been reclaimed for arable farming in keeping with the surrounding countryside. In 1987 American veterans returned to the village, were entertained, and left a Commemorative plaque in the Crown public house.

The village now has a population of about 400. Many old dwellings remain mainly round the church, and new developments have been small. Of the several farms in the parish only one is dairy, one has a farm shop and there is one pig and one poultry farm. A modern poultry-processing plant has recently been built within the boundary of the parish. Wormingford is fortunate to have a village shop with post office, a school, two public houses and a regular bus service to both Sudbury and Colchester.

The two public houses are of interest with the Crown being one of the ancient inns of Essex as its name appears as a landmark on deeds in 1691. In 1982 whilst extensive repairs were being carried out two mummified cats were found, one each side of the chimney. It was customary among cottage and inn builders in the Middle Ages to mummify a cat by burial alive in the walls to provide psychic protection. The cats date the inn to about 1600 when Elizabeth Newman, the Witch of Wormingford, was accused and tried for practising witchcraft. The pub was also a smithy in the 19th and 20th centuries.

Wrabness 🦜

Wrabness is a small village on high ground on the south bank of the river Stour. Its extent is about 1100 acres.

All Saints church overlooks the river and has several traces of its Norman origin, with two remarkable features in the porch. One is the arch over the inner doorway, which supports above it traces of another arch of Norman origin, the second is the 13th century stone coffin top, with a consecration cross, that has been inserted in the west wall.

The tower fell many years ago and a wooden belfry containing a single bell is now in the south west corner of the churchyard, covered with evergreen creeper. The date of the belfry may be 17th or 18th century and it is now a listed building which attracts much attention. The bell is rung every Sunday calling people to church.

On the north side of the churchyard there was once a schoolroom. There are no records of any burials on a piece of ground measuring 25 by 30 feet, where, it is said, the schoolroom stood, until it was pulled down and the rubble used to build the new school in 1872. Today the school has been converted into a house and both old and new rectories sold to private residents.

On an 18th century map there is a spot off the Ness named Cunningford Loading. Within living memory posts were still visible in the river where barges could be moored. Cargoes of baled hay and straw would be sent to London.

Writtle 🦜

Writtle is an ancient village with many interesting old buildings – and strangely it was from here that a part of the modern age began when the first wireless telephone broadcasts were made by Marconi.

One local resident is descended from the King family, who carried on a coal merchant's business in the village this century. She remembers: 'My grandfather and his family first lived at the Gas House, on St John's Green, which at that time had a tar pit, and a Chelmsford doctor would send his patients to walk around it as a cold cure.

The family later moved to Maltese House in Bridge Street. The horses were shod at either Pamplin's or Wallace's, blacksmiths in the village. Maltese House was originally part of the maltings. The family made the first floor into living quarters and the open spaces on ground level which had served as drying areas for the hops, were used as stables and coal storage.

From the windows of Maltese House could be seen the famous hut belonging to Marconi, where broadcasting first started in February 1922. One of the engineers working there married a local publican's daughter. Another had taken a fancy to a maid in one of the big houses, and the story goes that he would climb onto the roof of the hut with flags and send her a semaphore message. At a pre-arranged time, no doubt, she would be conveniently dusting her lady's bedroom and would answer with the wave of her duster from the open window.'

Castle Hedingham

Index